GodPRINTS

...ible FUNSTUFF

FUNTASTIC
KID
CRAFTS

By Susan Parsons
with
Lois Keffer

FUNtastic KidCrafts
Copyright © Susan Parsons

Published by Cook Communications Ministries

Printed in the United States

First printing, 2002
1 2 3 4 5 6 7 8 9 10 07 06 05 04 03 02

Edited by: Lois Keffer and Susan Martins Miller
Junior Creative Assistant: Aurora D. Parsons
Art Direction: Mike Riester and Scot McDonald
Cover Design: Peter Schmidt, Granite Design
Interior Design: Dana Sherrer, iDesignEtc.

ISBN: 0781438381

TABLE of CONTENTS

chapter FIVE Fashion Funnery

chapter SIX Tin Can-Its

chapter SEVEN Bugsies and Beasties—and Bears! Oh My!

INTRODUCTION

This book is your invitation to hours and hours of crafting fun for the kids in your children's ministry. Wait 'til you see the dawn of delight in your kids' eyes as they get their hands on these gooey, glitzy, FUNtastic projects. Besides the rewarding experience of making useful gifts, games and treasures from almost nothing, they'll learn about God in the process!

Each project gives you an opportunity to build godly character in your kids. Some encourage thoughtfulness and generosity through the making and giving of personal gifts. Cool things to wear help kids proclaim their faith. Games and goodies teach a media-minded generation that there's great fun to be had away from the TV or computer screen. Projects from recycled materials teach stewardship and resourcefulness. And with every craft, we've included a "Crafting Character" section to help kids apply biblical principles to their lives.

Next time someone tells you that crafting is mere child's play, remember that God himself is the original Creator. Throughout Scripture, skilled craftspersons are honored and their work given priority in the building and outfitting of the tabernacle and the temple.

So dig out your scissors and goodie box and get ready to be amazed at the wonderful things your kids create with FUNtastic KidCrafts!

As you get started with your crafting ministry, remember this special "crafter's blessing" from Scripture:

May the favor of the Lord our God rest upon us; establish
the work of our hands for us—yes, establish the work of our hands.
Psalm 90:17

In this chapter

Chapter 1
Nifty Gifties

The best gift is one from the heart. And that's where homemade gifts come from—straight from the heart with custom creativity!

This chapter offers gift ideas that are fun to make! They can be as easy or complex as your skill allows, with no difference in quality. For example, you can stencil the simple gift bags with basic geometric shapes or with your own intricate design. Either way, your gift bags will look like they could come right out of a specialty gift store.

Enjoy making these nifty and inexpensive gifts, and bless someone special!

Borax Crystal Ornaments

These crystal-spangled sparklers will help kids see that, like gemstones, they are precious in God's sight.

1. Cut a chenille wire into three sections. Twist two sections together to form an X. Then twist the third section to form six even arms. Arrange them so they're evenly spaced.

2. Cut the other chenille wire into 2-inch pieces. Wrap each piece around the end of an arm so it looks like a three-tined fork.

3. Tie string to the center of one of the arms, stretch it to the next arm and wrap it around, then to the next, until it forms a "circle" in the snowflake.

4. Tie one end of a 6-inch string to one of the arms; tie the other end to a pencil.

5. Pour one cup of boiling water at a time into a wide mouth jar (wider than the snowflake). Add 3 tablespoons of borax per cup of water in the jar and stir. Some settling of granules is normal.

6. Drop the snowflake into the mix and rest the pencil across the mouth of the jar. The snowflake needs to "float" off the bottom of the jar so that crystals may form.

By morning, your snowflake will be covered with jewel-like crystals!

YOU'LL NEED:

- **Borax laundry booster such as 20 Mule-Team Borax®** (be careful not to buy a borax-based detergent by mistake)
- **String**
- **Jar**
- **Boiling water**
- **Pencil or stick**
- **White chenille wires (2 per snowflake)**

If you just can't stop here…
Let kids make ornaments in other shapes. They may want to form their initials, a heart, a tree or flower. The only limit is what will fit in the jar! You can experiment with color by adding a few drops of food coloring to the hot water.

GODPRINT: Preciousness

CRAFTING CHARACTER

BIBLE VERSE: *As you come to him [Jesus], the living Stone—rejected by men but chosen by God and precious to him— you also, like living stones, are being built into a spiritual house to be a holy priesthood.* (1 Peter 2:4–5).

• What do you think will happen to the chenille wire after it's been in the jar for a while?

Borax crystals will form overnight as the water cools. But the crystals that make up certain precious stones are formed over thousands of years through heat and pressure. That's what makes them so precious.

• Who can name some precious stones? *(Diamonds, emeralds, rubies.)*

• Do you see any precious stones in our room? *(Someone might be wearing a diamond engagement ring.)*
• Why are people willing to pay a lot of money for precious stones? *(They're beautiful; as gifts, they show how much someone cares.)*

Did you know that you're precious? More precious than any gem! The Bible says that you're a *living* stone that helps make up God's church. Ask a volunteer to read 1 Peter 2:4–5. **Precious stones become beautiful in the heat and pressure of the earth. People aren't all that different. When we go through the heat of pain and hard times, we learn to depend on God. Then God works in us to develop his own beautiful character. We become the living stones that make up his kingdom on earth. How's that for special?**

EZ Memo Board

A bright memo board can serve as a memory tickler to help kids track chores and celebrate their accomplishments.

1. Cut a rectangle (11"x15" or the size of your choice) from cardboard or foamcore. Cut a piece of batting the same size.

2. Cut a 15"x19" piece of fabric (or any size that extends two inches beyond each edge of the board). Kids love being able to choose, so have three or four patterned fabrics for kids to choose from.

3. Place the fabric face down. Center the batting on the fabric, then add the cardboard. Wrap the fabric to the back of the cardboard as if you were wrapping a package. Pin or hot glue it into place.

4. Turn the board over. Weave ribbons across the front, as shown in the photo. Secure them on the back with straight pins pushed in at an angle. Boys might prefer using jute twine.

5. Tuck "To-Do" notes and favorite Bible verses under the ribbons, along with keepsakes and pictures of friends!

YOU'LL NEED:

- Cardboard or foamcore
- Fabric
- Quilt batting
- Hot glue gun or pins
- Satin ribbon or jute twine
- Bright colored sticky notes

If you just can't stop here…
Add a fun memento of your memo-board-making project by taking individual and group photos of your kids as they work. Next week, give everyone copies of the photos to add to their memo boards. Better yet, take instant photos or do printouts from a digital camera so kids can take their memo boards home loaded with good memories!

GoDPRINT: Service

CRAFTING CHARACTER

BIBLE VERSE: *Whatever you do, work at it with all your heart, as working for the Lord, not for men, since you know that you will receive an inheritance from the Lord as a reward. It is the Lord Christ you are serving* (Colossians 3:23–24).

• What chores are you responsible for each week?
• How do you remember to get them done?

What can you do when chores turn into a bore? Get a whole new attitude about them! Listen carefully to this Bible passage, and see if you can discover what kind of attitude adjustment I'm talking about. Have a volunteer read Colossians 3:23–24.

• How can something like taking out the garbage or feeding the dog be like serving Christ?

• How does it feel to take charge of your chores, rather than having someone nag you into doing them?

Hand out sticky notes. Encourage kids to copy Colossians 3:23–24 onto one note. Have them write their weekly chores on other notes.

• How can you arrange these notes on your board to keep yourself on the ball?

It's a great feeling when you take charge of things and get yourself organized! And a really cool benefit of staying on top of your responsibilities is that you earn your parents' appreciation and respect. You'll be amazed at what an impact your helpful, servant attitude can have on your family. Give it a month and watch what happens. When you do what's right before the Lord, lots of people benefit!

Memourri Potpourri

Little bowls of colorful, sweet "scentiment" make great gifts and remembrances for all kinds of special days.

1. Plan to begin this project one or two weeks ahead of time. (What a good idea for the waiting period of Advent!) Let everyone work together to prepare the botanicals for drying. Remove petals from flowers. Cut very thin slices of apple and orange—be sure to include the peel.

2. Place botanicals of similar weight in brown paper bags or between paper towels. Dry them in the microwave at 50% power for about five minutes. Check the moisture level of the materials and run the oven again if necessary. Let kids prepare another batch of botanicals while the first one is in the oven. To process several batches in one session, ask a helper to bring in a portable microwave oven.

3. Spoon the mixture into zip-top bags. Leave room for shaking!

4. Let kids choose from woodsy and floral scented oils. Supervise as they add about 10 drops of oil to their bags. (Remember that these oils are strong enough to ruin a varnished or enameled finish, so be careful not to set a drippy vial on the church piano!)

5. Put on some lively music and shake, shake, shake! This will distribute the oils throughout the potpourri.

YOU'LL NEED:

- Your choice of "botanicals" such as flower petals from a special bouquet, pine needles, thin apple and orange slices, bay leaves, geranium, lavender, sage, and small pine cones
- Cutting board and knife (and an adult!)
- Zip-top bags
- Scented oils
- Microwave oven
- Paper towels
- Paper bags

6. The next week, add a few more drops of oil and shake again. If possible, let the potpourri "ripen" one more week.

If you just can't stop here...
Create woodsy gift sachets by cutting rectangles from brown paper bags and folding them to create packets. Or, use decorative envelopes. Place potpourri inside and tie the sachet with jute or plaid ribbon. For extra charm, add a couple of cinnamon sticks to the bow.

GODPRINT: Confidence

CRAFTING CHARACTER

BIBLE VERSE: *He has made everything beautiful in its time. He has also set eternity in the hearts of men; yet they cannot fathom what God has done from beginning to end* (Ecclesiastes 3:11).

- What do you think would have happened if we hadn't waited a few days for our potpourri to be ready?
- When is it really hard for you to wait? For your birthday? For Christmas? To eat something that's baking and smells really good?

Ask a volunteer to read Ecclesiastes 3:11. **God's people waited a long time for Jesus to come to earth. Hundreds and hundreds of years. And during those years of waiting, they had to endure a lot of hard times. Their country was defeated and their cities destroyed. They had to go off and live as slaves in a foreign land. At times, they must have wondered if their waiting would ever come to an end. But during those years, prophets reminded them of God's faithfulness. And so they kept patiently waiting until Jesus was finally born.**

- Who can tell me how Jesus was different from the king God's people had been expecting?

Jesus truly was a beautiful Savior. Instead of ruling over a tiny kingdom in the Mideast, he rules over people's hearts, forever! And the fragrance of his love fills our lives today! God doesn't always do things the way we would. But in his time, he makes everything beautiful. It's our job to live for him patiently and expectantly, and watch for all the beautiful things he does!

Foamie Frames

This cute-as-a-button frame project leads to a thoughtful discussion about how we can choose to rely on God to help us discern right from wrong.

1. Let kids choose two contrasting colors of craft foam. Help them measure and cut one 5" x 7" piece to form the backing of the frame. Cut the other piece to measure 4" x 6".

2. Help kids fold the smaller piece in half without creasing it, and cut a rectangle out of the fold, leaving a frame that's one inch wide.

3. Open the frame and apply a thin bead of glue at the outer edge on three sides. Be sure to leave the top unglued. Center the frame piece onto the backing and press it firmly into place.

4. Glue on colorful buttons to decorate the frame.

5. Create a stand by cutting a strip of foam 2 1/2" wide and 5" long. Lay the strip vertically on the back of the frame so that the bottom edges line up. Glue the top one-inch of the strip to the frame.

6. When it dries, glue one end of a 2 1/2" piece of ribbon to the back of the frame under the strip, and the other end to the inside of the strip. The ribbon will keep the stand from opening too far.

YOU'LL NEED:

- **Sheets of craft foam**
- **Glue**
- **Colorful buttons**
- **Ribbon**

If you just can't stop here...
Choose a fun computer font and print out Psalm 25:4–5 in a 4"x 6" box. Let kids cut out and decorate the verse, then place it in their frames.

GODPRINT: Discernment

CRAFTING CHARACTER

BIBLE VERSE: *Show me your ways, O LORD, teach me your paths; guide me in your truth and teach me, for you are God my Savior, and my hope is in you all day long* (Psalm 25:4–5).

• When you take your frame home, how will you decide what picture to put in it?

You might choose a picture of your family or a friend or a pet. Or you could choose a picture that has colors that look nice with the colors of your frame. Deciding what to put in your frame is a fun, easy choice. But sometimes the choices we have to make aren't fun or easy. That's when we need God's help.

King David must have been facing a difficult choice when he wrote this prayer.
Have a volunteer read Psalm 25:4–5.

• Who can tell about a time when you relied on God's help to make a hard choice, or tell the difference between right and wrong?

God gives us his Holy Spirit to help us make good choices. When we ask, we can count on God to help us judge when something is true or false, pure or impure, good or evil. When we tune in to God, he helps us understand what's good for us and what's not.

• Would anyone like to talk about a difficult choice you're facing right now?
• How can David's prayer help you?

There's no better "coach" in life than God himself. Learn to rely on him when you have choices to make. God won't let you down!

Bath Salts

Incredibly soothing and fragrant, these bath salts make a thoughtful gift that adults will appreciate!

1. Set out mixing bowls and pour Epsom salts into each bowl.

2. Let kids have fun mixing various fragrance oils and food coloring in the different bowls. Offer oils such as vanilla, eucalyptus, lavender and birch. Essential oils are extremely potent. Coach kids to stir in just a few drops at a time.

3. Have kids spoon the mixed salts into jars.

4. Coat the tops of the jar lids with glue, then led kids decorate them with coiled twine, pine cones, fabric or plastic beads and gems.

5. Tie ribbon or twine around the edge of the lid.

YOU'LL NEED:

- Epsom salts
- Mixing bowls
- Food coloring
- Scented oils
- Wooden or plastic spoons
- Small glass jars
- Ribbon or twine
- Glue
- Your choice of twine, pine cones, fabric or plastic beads and gems

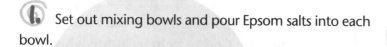

If you just can't stop here…

Let kids cut and fold nice paper to make gift tags to tie onto their jars. Have them copy this rhyme onto their tags: "Take a nice, long soak today. Let your troubles float away!"

GODPRINT: Empathy

CRAFTING CHARACTER

BIBLE VERSE: *Then Mary took about a pint of pure nard, an expensive perfume; she poured it on Jesus' feet and wiped his feet with her hair. And the house was filled with the fragrance of the perfume* (John 12:3).

• On a scale of 1 to 10, how rushed and busy has life been at your house this week?

• How can you tell when your mom or dad is stressed because there's so much to do?

One sign of up growing up is learning to be aware of the feelings of people around you. When we're aware of what others are going through, we can respond to them in ways that show God's love. That's what Mary did for Jesus in today's Bible passage. Ask a volunteer to read John 12:1–8. **Think how busy and stressful Jesus' life must have been! When this dinner happened, Jesus knew that the time for him to die was coming. The special honor and care that Mary gave Jesus brought him comfort.**

• What are some special things you can do for your parents to show that you understand and care about how they feel?

Sometimes a small, well-timed act of kindness can become an unforgettable experience. Maybe it would take only fifteen minutes for you to do extra chores one evening and give Mom or Dad a chance to escape and soak away their cares in a hot bath.

• When would be a good time to do this act of kindness at your house?

Give kids newspaper or grocery bags to use to take their bath salts home. Encourage them to be aware of their parents' feelings and pass on their fragrant gifts at a time that will bring comfort.

That's A Wrap!

Handmade wrapping paper is the perfect packaging for handmade gifts and crafts. It carries the personal touch a little further. And it's easy!

1. You may want to ask volunteers to collect and bring several grocery bags apiece for this project. Show kids how to cut a clean rectangle from a grocery bag by cutting down the back seam, then trimming away the bottom edge.

2. Let kids pour acrylic paint onto paper plates. Supervise carefully as they add a few drops of water to each plate and stir it to thin the paint slightly.

3. While some kids are pouring and stirring paint, let others cut sponges into fun shapes such as stripes, squiggles, bows or dots.

4. Show kids how to dip sponges into paint, scrape the excess on the side of the plate, and sponge the patterns randomly over their papers.

5. Let them add tiny dots of glitter glue for sparkle.

6. Make sure kids write their initials in the corner of each sheet of paper they complete. Set the sponged gift wrap aside to dry. Shortcut!: If you're in a hurry, have a helper blow dry the finished papers.

YOU'LL NEED:

- Brown paper grocery bags
- Scissors
- Acrylic paint
- Paper plates
- Sponges
- Glitter glue

If you just can't stop here…

There are so many great ways to decorate wrapping paper. Use rubber stamps. Use a toothbrush dipped in thin paint to spatter over well-formed leaves. Bundle several markers with a rubber band and make rainbow squiggles.

GODPRINT: Discipleship

CRAFTING CHARACTER

BIBLE VERSE: *And we, who with unveiled faces all reflect the Lord's glory, are being transformed into his likeness with ever-increasing glory, which comes from the Lord, who is the Spirit* (2 Corinthians 3:18).

Hold up a slightly crumpled brown grocery bag.

• Do you think this is a thing of beauty?
• Would anyone pay me a dollar for it? Why not?

Hold up a couple of the decorated papers kids made.

• What about these? What makes these worth more than this plain bag?
• Why would someone be excited to get a gift wrapped in this paper?

It's been fun to watch you transform something plain into something so beautiful and personal. That reminds me of what God does in the lives of people who love him. We invested a little time in making these plain bags beautiful. God invested in us, too. He sent his own son, Jesus, to be our Savior. As we learn to know God, we begin to see how great and wonderful and loving he is. The more we know about him and spend time with him in prayer, the more he works in our lives. The Bible says he changes us to be like him. Have a volunteer read 2 Corinthians 3:18.

• Have you ever seen God work in someone's life? How did that person change?
• How do you feel God working in your life to help you become more like him?

When you see yourself in the mirror this week, remind yourself that you're a work of art in progress, and God is the artist!

Bag-Its!

A few quick tricks with a
lunch bag and you have a great
gift container for treats and crafts!

1. Help kids cut off the tops of their bags with pinking shears or other scissors with a fancy edge.

2. Fold the top of the bag down one inch. Punch two holes near the center, about an inch apart.

3. Let kids decorate the bag. They may want to write the recipient's name in glitter glue. (Let a helper speed-dry the glitter glue with a blow dryer.) See the "That's A Wrap" craft on page 18 for lots of decorating ideas.

4. Place in the bag whatever crafts or goodies you've prepared.

5. Fold the top over again. Let kids choose from a variety of ribbon or raffia and push the ends through the holes from back to front.

6. Tie the ribbon with streamers hanging down.

YOU'LL NEED:

- Paper lunch bags
- Pinking shears
- Ribbon
- Hole punch
- Glitter glue
- Optional: blow dryer

If you just can't stop here…
Let kids add fun extras to the bow, such as jingle bells, strands of curling ribbon, notes of appreciation, or wrapped candies.

GODPRINT: Kindness

CRAFTING CHARACTER

BIBLE VERSE: *Therefore, as God's chosen people, holy and dearly loved, clothe yourselves with compassion, kindness, humility, gentleness and patience* (Colossians 3:12).

• When you get a fancy little package like this, what do you expect to find inside it? Why?

In the Bible, God tells us over and over not to worry so much about what we're like on the outside, but to focus instead on what we're like on this inside. Listen very carefully as we read about how God wants us to "clothe ourselves." Have a volunteer read Colossians 3:12.

• How are you supposed to clothe yourself with all those good things?
• What is God's part in getting us dressed in compassion, kindness, humility, gentleness and patience?
• Which is the most challenging for you to "put on"?

Let each student take an extra length of ribbon. **Tie your ribbon through a belt loop or button hole. Let it serve to remind you that God has some extra special "wrappings" for you.**

• Who can name the wrappings God wants us to put on?

It's fun to work with you and see what great packages God is making of your lives!

As kids are making their bags and wrapping, ask some questions:
• What's special about a hand-made gift? *(Help kids understand that a hand-made gift shows that they have not only spent money, but time and care in making the gift. They are sharing their gift of creativity with others.)*

• What should our attitude be when we give? *(We should delight in giving! We should never feel obligated to give a gift, because then we will resent it. God loves a cheerful giver: "Each man should give what he has decided in his heart to give, not reluctantly or under compulsion, for God loves a cheerful giver" 2 Corinthians 9:7.)*

In this chapter

Chapter 2
Tom-Toolery

Everybody has a junk drawer or two. Or five. Maybe even a junk closet, or a junk ROOM! Take a look at what's hiding in yours. Old tools? Pieces of hardware you never used when you put up the blinds? Old nuts and bolts and screws?

Gather up these treasures! You're about to use them as you engage in a little Tom-Toolery!

You'll be surprised what you can make from junk and how useful—and in some cases, beautiful—these items can be! Let this chapter teach your kids—and you—a few things about resourcefulness! Enjoy!

Nutty Necklaces

Nutty because they're made from nuts, or because they're so whimsical? You decide! Meanwhile, you should be aware that this craft is one of the easier nuts to crack!

1. Let each child choose assorted nuts and arrange them on newspaper the way they'd like their necklaces to look.

2. As kids are arranging their necklaces, pour different colors of acrylic paints into plastic margarine tubs. Also set out bowls of clear water for cleaning brushes.

3. Let kids paint the sides of the nuts in different colors. When they're dry, roll them over and paint the underside as well.

4. Starting from the nut on the far left, string the nuts in order from left to right.

5. Tie the ends of elastic together for a stretchy necklace. If you're using leather shoelaces, tie knots in each end to keep the nuts from slipping off.

YOU'LL NEED:

- Metal nuts in various sizes
- Newspapers
- Elastic string or leather bootlace
- Acrylic paints
- Plastic margarine tubs
- Small paint brushes

If you just can't stop here...

Tie a thread to each nut and dip it in white glue, followed by a good dunking in tiny beads or "bead glitter"—packets or vials of these are usually in the glitter section of your craft store. Regular glitter can be messy, as the glitter may rub off on your clothing. Let the nuts dry thoroughly by hanging them by their threads on a clothesline or hanger before the final stringing. Cut the temporary thread and string your lovely, nutty beads! Gorgeous, dahling!

GODPRINT: Obedience

CRAFTING CHARACTER

BIBLE VERSE: *My son, keep your father's commands and do not forsake your mother's teaching. Bind them upon your heart forever; fasten them around your neck* (Proverbs 6:20–21).

• How many of you have ever helped to train a dog?
• What are some of the things that it's important for a dog to learn? Why?
• What are some bad habits that you've seen in dogs?

Hold up one of the necklaces the kids made. **Your cool-looking "nutty necklaces" remind me that a collar is an important tool in training a dog. A little tug on a collar helps a dog pay attention and keeps it from wandering into dangerous places. It takes a lot of patience and love to train a dog properly. It takes even more patience to train kids to make wise choices.**

• What are some of the first things your parents taught you to keep you safe when you were little?
• What are some of the rules they give you now?
• How do you feel about those rules?

Believe it or not, it's a lot more trouble to train kids and give them good rules than to let them do whatever they want to do. Have a volunteer read Proverbs 6:20–21. **Let your "nutty" necklace be a reminder of all the good things your parents do to teach you to be safe. Rules aren't meant to keep you from having fun. They're meant to guide you toward a wonderful, happy life. Next time your parents give you a little "tug," thank them!**

Grubber Band Clan

Kids learn how fun resourcefulness can be when they put these great puppets together from toolroom junk!

1. Help each kid select an old tool for the head of a "grublet" puppet—a big old paintbrush, wide putty knife, even a whisk broom will work. Grubby stains and splatter just add individuality to your grublet!

2. Search through your tool box, basement or junk drawers for objects to use for the eyes and nose. Some examples include nuts, washers, rubber rings, etc. If possible, ask kids to bring some items from their junk drawers at home. Set out all the items where kids can choose freely.

3. Show kids how to place the rubber band where the mouth should be. Lay it so that the flattest, or least curved, part of the rubber band forms the upper lip (i.e., so that the curves form the corners of the mouth).

4. Glue only the upper lip of the mouth to the grublet's face. Glue all other facial parts evenly.

5. After the glue has dried thoroughly, tie a long thread to the center of the lower lip (rubber band). Run it through the handle hole, if there is one (this just hides the thread a bit more). When you pull the thread, the mouth will open! Give it slack, and the mouth will pop closed again!

YOU'LL NEED:

- Old paintbrushes, putty spreaders or feather dusters
- Small rubber bands (thicker is better)
- Odds and ends from your toolbox—be creative and resourceful!
- E-6000® adhesive (hot glue will not work on metal surfaces)
- Strands of thread

If you just can't stop there…
Nail carpet tacks to the sides of the wooden handles near the "head." Tie rubber-tube arms to the tacks with fishing line. Glue on hands made of whatever toolroom junk you can find! Attach thin dowels to the "hands" to move the arms. Add aluminum foil clothing, if desired.

GODPRINT: Resourcefulness

CRAFTING CHARACTER

BIBLE VERSE: *She gets up while it is still dark; she provides food for her family and portions for her servant girls. She considers a field and buys it; out of her earnings she plants a vineyard. She sets about her work vigorously, her arms are strong for her tasks* (Proverbs 31:15–17).

If you were stranded on a deserted island, what would you do for food and shelter? Let kids give their ideas.

Your ideas are examples of *resourcefulness*. If you were stranded on an island, resourcefulness would help you build a shelter out of whatever materials you could find. Resourcefulness would help you find food to eat that you wouldn't normally think of. Resourcefulness can help people through emergencies, or save money. Whatever abilities you have, you can use them to accomplish a job that God gives you to do.

• How were we resourceful in making these puppets? *(Thought of our own ideas; used junk instead of buying new things.)*

• How did being resourceful solve some of the problems we ran into?

Many of the people in the Bible were resourceful. Let's read about one of them. Ask a volunteer to Read Proverbs 31:15–17.

• How did this woman show that she was resourceful?
• How can resourcefulness help your family save money?
• What skills can you learn to help you be more resourceful at home?

The woman in Proverbs thought carefully about what she needed to do and planned ahead. She used what she had to provide for her family, then bought a field and planted a vineyard to make the most of the field.

When you run into a problem this week and think you don't have what you need to solve the problem, remember this woman from Proverbs. Ask God to show you some ideas you didn't think of on your own.

Surging Waters Bracelets

Wearing these miniature typhoons can remind kids that Jesus promised to be with us through every storm.

1. For each child, cut a 1-inch piece of the 3/4-inch tubing.

2. Each child will need a length of the 1/2-inch-wide tubing to fit around his or her wrist—don't forget it has to slide over the hand, too.

3. Put a dab of adhesive around one end of the bracelet tube, and slip the small, 1-inch piece around it.

4. Pair up kids and show them how to plug up the fat end of a friend's tube with a finger while the friend fills the tube with bubble solution to 1 inch from the top. Remind kids to add some glitter and sequins.

5. Show how to put some glue around the other end of the bracelet and *carefully* connect the ends. Shake the glitter so it mixes well and creates bubbles in the solution.

6. Remind kids to let the bracelet dry completely (a couple of hours) before trying to put it on!

YOU'LL NEED:

- E-6000® adhesive
- Clear plastic tubing, 3/4 inch wide
- Clear plastic tubing, 1/2 inch wide
- Bubble solution (or mixture of water and clear dishwashing liquid or shampoo)
- Glitter, small metallic sequins
- Optional: Food coloring

If you just can't stop here…
Make matching necklaces!

GODPRINT: Trust

BIBLE VERSE: *God is our refuge and strength, an ever-present help in trouble. Therefore we will not fear, though the earth give way and the mountains fall into the heart of the sea, though its waters roar and foam and the mountains quake with their surging* (Psalm 46:1–3).

- How many of you have been swimming in an ocean? What did that feel like?
- What makes it hard to swim in the waves of the ocean? Can you swim in the opposite direction of the waves?

The foamy waters of a crashing sea can make us think about the hard time we have in our lives. Sometimes it seems as if we're trying to swim against the strong waves.

- What are some things that make you afraid?

CRAFTING CHARACTER

- If you have someone with you, is it easier or harder to face hard things?

We all have troubles, but we don't have to fear those troubles. That's because God promised to help us *through* them. Ask a volunteer to read Psalm 46:1–3.

- What is a "refuge"? (*A place to go for help or protection.*)
- What does "ever-present help" mean?

Move your bracelet around and see what happens to the water.

- How can this bracelet remind you to trust God when you have stormy times?

Wear your "surging waters" bracelet and remember that God is with you as you weather the storms of your life.

Lightbulb Finial Ornaments

Talk about the beauty of God's never-ending light while fashioning these elegant finial ornaments from blown bulbs!

1. Show kids how to tie a long string tightly around the neck of the bulb.

2. Mix a few tablespoons of white glue with a few drops of water in a bowl.

3. Explain how to paint the entire glass portion of the bulb liberally with glue while holding on to the metal part. Remind them to keep the string out of the glue.

4. Have kids hold the bulb over a paper plate and cover it with glitter. Shake off the excess, then hang the bulb by the string to dry, untouched, for an hour.

5. Meanwhile, kids can paint the squirt-bottle cap with metallic paint. Some of them may want to cover the sides with velvet or satin ribbon and add a tassel to the tip. When the bulb is dry, kids can center and glue the rim of the squirt cap to the bottom of the bulb. Continue decorating the bulb with vertical ribbons, sequins, etc.

YOU'LL NEED:

- Lightbulbs—standard and vanity (round) style
- Squirt-bottle caps of all kinds
- Large cans of glitter
- Craft glue
- Paintbrushes
- Water
- Small bowl
- Your choice of sequins, satin ribbons, metallic trims, small tassels and beads
- Gold or silver paint or markers

6. Remove the string. Glue a five-inch loop of ribbon to each side of the neck.

7. Glue ribbon or cording around the neck of the bulb. Let it dry, then hang it!

If you just can't stop here…
Use different kinds of bulbs for a variety of shapes.

GODPRINT: Wonder

CRAFTING CHARACTER

BIBLE VERSE: *Your word is a lamp to my feet and a light for my path* (Psalm 119:105).

• When you enter a dark room, what's the first thing you do? *(Flip the switch and turn on the light.)*
• What about when you walk around outside at night, like on a camping trip? *(Use a flashlight or lantern.)*
• Why are some people afraid of the dark? How does a nightlight help?
• What do room lights and flashlights have in common. *(Light bulbs.)*

Light bulbs are useful tools. They help us to see in the dark. Before the light bulb was invented, people used candles, oil lamps or gas lights to help them see. We keep finding better ways to light up what's around us.

The Bible says that God's Word is a light.

Ask a volunteer to read Psalm 119:105.

• How does this verse say that God's Word helps us?
• What happens if you have no light and can't see the path your feet should be on?

A light reveals things we can't see in the dark. Without the Bible, we're "in the dark" about how God wants us to live. All we have to do to turn on the light of God's Word is read it! God tells us what kinds of people he wants us to be and how to be close to him.

We used old, burned-out light bulbs to make our ornaments. But God's light never burns out. It doesn't burn down like a candle. It doesn't run out of oil like an oil lamp. It keeps on shining. When you look at your ornament, remember that God's Word stays bright in our hearts!

Bulb-u-ous Penguin

Illustrate the concept of disguising or "covering up" our sins with this wonderful penguin made from an old light bulb!

1. Show kids how to paint the light bulb black except for a pear-shaped portion of the belly section (below the neck). Set the bulb on the tissue roll stand to dry. When the black paint has dried, paint the pear-shaped belly space white.

2. Cut a long strip of felt 1/2-inch wide for each scarf. Let the kids tie scarves around their penguins' necks and trim them for the desired length. If they'd like, kids can "fringe" the ends.

3. Cut a 3-inch triangle of felt for the hat. Fold two sides together and glue them to form a stocking cap. Add a felt "ball" to the point or use a bead.

4. Glue the hat to the top of the penguin's head and the wiggly eyes to the face. Cut a tiny, carrot-shaped piece of orange or yellow felt and glue it just below the eyes. Cut two black felt flippers and glue them to the sides.

5. Cut two almond-shaped feet (about an inch long each) and glue them in a "V" shape to a small piece of cardboard. Cut the cardboard into a single piece to fit the feet and hot glue it to the bulb.

Optional: Ask some older kids to help you cut out all the felt shapes you'll need ahead of time in an assortment of colors.

YOU'LL NEED:

- Standard light bulbs
- Black and white paint
- Paintbrushes
- Felt scraps
- Hot glue gun and glue sticks
- Cardboard scraps
- Empty bathroom tissue rolls, cut to 2-inches
- Wiggly craft eyes

If you just can't stop here...
Try making some other characters with light bulbs! Bulbs make great snowmen, Santas, bears and moose! Experiment and see what else you can come up with!

GODPRINT: Honesty

CRAFTING CHARACTER

BIBLE VERSE: *My eyes are on all their ways; they are not hidden from me, nor is their sin concealed from my eyes* (Jeremiah 16:17).

Wow! We've really transformed these light bulbs. A penguin is nothing like a light bulb, but we've kind of hidden the bulb in all the penguin decorations.

• Do you think people will be able to tell there's a bulb under all the decorations? Why or why not?

People will be surprised when you tell them that your penguin is really a disguised light bulb.

• Can you think of some other things that are easy to disguise or hide?
• Tell me about something that is impossible to disguise or hide.

Lots of things are easy to disguise and change. But God can never be fooled. We can't hide our sin. Ask a volunteer to read Jeremiah 16:17.

• Tell me in your own words what you think this verse means.
• Name some ways that people try to hide their sins.

Being honest means that we are truthful. God wants us to be truthful because he is truthful. We can lie to someone by what we say or do, or we can lie by what we leave out and what we don't do. If we lie, we might be able to fool some people. But no matter how we try to cover our sins by lying, cheating or sneaking around, we don't fool God.

When you look at your penguin, and see the penguin looking back at you with his wiggly eyes, you'll know there's a light bulb hidden in the penguin. I hope that will help you remember that you can't hide anything from God.

In this chapter

Chapter 3
Rag-Tag Toys

There's something especially rewarding about playing with a toy you made by yourself! And being able to make your own new toys can come in handy during those long waits between birthdays and Christmas!

So save your cereal boxes, shoe boxes, old plastic straws, colorful socks and plastic grocery bags. All of them can become treasured toys in a matter of minutes!

Prayer-A-Chute

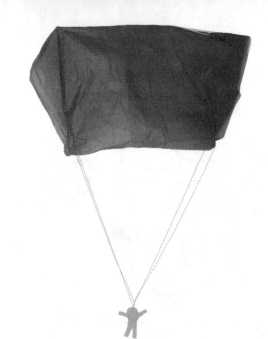

Blessings come down as your prayers go up! That's the message attached to this fun favorite of boys and girls alike!

1. Cut a plastic bag into an 18-inch square.

2. Show how to poke a tiny hole in each corner, about 1/2 inch from the edges.

3. Give each child four 18-inch lengths of fishing line. Run one length through each corner hole and knot securely.

4. Attach the metal washer to the four pieces of fishing line. Make sure the pieces of fishing line are equal in length when tied.

5. Encourage kids to throw the prayer-a-chute high into the air and watch it drift down!

YOU'LL NEED:

- Plastic bags
- Fishing line
- 3/4-inch metal washer
- Optional: construction paper for the body

If you just can't stop here...

Experiment with cardboard or foamie characters of different weights. Keep the characters small—just a couple of inches tall. If he's too light, make a larger paratrooper, or tape a stack of foamie squares to his back as a backpack!

GODPRINT: Prayerfulness

CRAFTING CHARACTER

BIBLE VERSE: *And pray in the Spirit on all occasions with all kinds of prayers and requests. With this in mind, be alert and always keep on praying for all the saints* (Ephesians 6:18).

• Have you ever seen someone in the air with a parachute?

• What do people use parachutes for? *(Jumping from a plane.)*

Sometimes people use parachutes because they love the feeling of floating in the air. Sometimes people use parachutes because it would be dangerous to stay in the plane if something went wrong with a plane. Sometimes people use parachutes when they want to come from the air and land in a certain place on the ground.

• How is prayer like a parachute?

We send our prayers up to God, and the answers come down! Ask a volunteer to read Ephesians 6:18.

• According to this verse, when should we pray? *(On all occasions.)*
• And what should we pray for? *(All kinds of prayers and requests.)*
• And who should we pray for? *(All the saints. Other believers.)*

Let's uses our prayer-a-chutes to do just what the verse says to do. Give each child two small slips of paper and a pencil. **On one piece of paper, write a prayer request for yourself. Then talk to a friend and find out how you can pray for another person. Write that prayer request on the second piece of paper. Then we'll tape both papers to our prayer-a-chutes.** Older kids can help younger kids with writing and taping.

Take turns having kids toss their prayer-a-chutes high in the air. As each one floats down, lead the group in saying, "Lord, hear our prayers." If you have access to a balcony or other elevated platform, try taking the group there to let them drop their chutes and watch them float down.

Fun Fishies

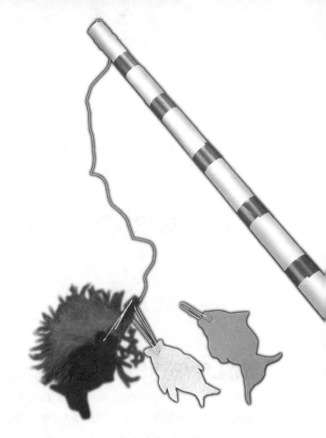

A fun accompaniment to a "fishers of men" story, this fishin' pole and these craft-foam fishies will give hours of fun!

1. Draw several fish on the craft foam (no larger than 2- or 3- inches long each) and cut them out. Older kids may want to help draw and cut fish for younger kids.

2. Use a hole punch to make a hole in the fish's mouth.

3. Open a paper clip end slightly and guide it through the fish's mouth, like putting a key on a key ring.

4. Cut two 2-inch strips from the magnet tape (or cut two pieces 3/4" x 2"). Show how to peel off the backing and stick the two pieces together with one end of the string between them.

5. Attach a feather just above the magnet (tie it or tape it) and wrap a small piece of chenille wire around it to form a lure "head."

6. Ask kids to tie the other end of the string to the dowel (or poster board rolled as tightly as possible and secured with stripes made from colorful electrical tape).

7. Let the kids drop the "bait" into the pile of fish and pull 'em in, one by one!

YOU'LL NEED:

- Craft foam
- Scissors
- Jumbo metal paperclips
- Dowels or sticks about 18" long (or roll a piece of poster board)
- 2-1/2 foot lengths of string or yarn (elastic string is the most fun!)
- Magnet tape or sheets
- Feathers
- Chenille wires
- Hole punch

If you just can't stop here…

Add a reel to your rod! This will only work with the poster board-tube rod. Use an empty craft-ribbon spool, a plastic straw and two 2-inch brads. Using the brad, attach the spool to the side of the rod "handle." Cut a 1-inch piece from the plastic straw. Run a brad through the straw piece and on through the spool, about 1 inch from the edge. Use a hole punch to punch a hole in the top of the rod. Now run a string through that hole, and draw it down to the spool. Tie it tightly around the spool, then wind the spool until you have the length of string you desire for the rod and reel. Kids will love pulling in their fish the "reel" way.

GODPRINT: Evangelism

CRAFTING CHARACTER

BIBLE VERSE: *"Come, follow me,"* *Jesus said, "and I will make you fishers of men"* (Matthew 4:19).

Jesus spent a lot of time around the Sea of Galilee. Many of the people who lived around the lake made their living by fishing. When Jesus began to find the people who would be his disciples, he went to the Sea of Galilee. That's where he found Peter and Andrew. What do you suppose they were doing? Fishing!

Peter and Andrew were great fishermen. They knew what nets to use and where to throw them and how to drag them in. But when Jesus found them that day, he had a brand new idea for them. Ask a volunteer to read Matthew 4:19.

• What did Jesus tell Peter and Andrew to do? *(Follow him.)*
• What did he promise them? *(That he would make them fishers of men.)*

• Have you ever wondered what those first disciples did to fish for people?

When you go fishing, you find water, right? That's where the fish will be. Jesus went to where he knew Peter and Andrew would be, and fishing for people means going to where the people will be.

Another thing you do when you go fishing is use a bait that is attractive to the fish. Some fishermen know just exactly what bait to use to make the kind of fish they want come to them.

• How can our words make people want to come to Jesus?
• How can our actions make people want to come to Jesus?

When you use your fishing pole, let it remind you that Jesus wants you to fish for people too! Tell the good news of Jesus to people who need to hear it.

Little Red Wagon

Kids can learn to "bear one another's burdens" while making their very own little red wagons to help dolls and teddy bears in need!

1. Show kids how to glue the top of the shoe box lid to the underside of the box.

2. Pass around hole punches so kids can make holes in the sides of the lid that form the "skirt" around the bottom of the wagon. Make the holes about two inches from the front and back ends of the wagon.

3. Using a large jar lid, compass or other circle template, trace four circles onto the cardboard. These are the wheels. Older kids can help younger kids who may not know how to use a compass. Push a metal brad through the very center of each circle, and then through a corresponding hole in the side of the wagon "skirt" and spread the brad to fasten it.

4. Cut a cardboard "T" about 12-inches long and two inches wide, with a 2" x 3" rectangle at the top of the "T." Cut out the center of the rectangle to form a handle.

5. Make a hole at the other end of the "T." Push a brad through the front center floor of the wagon, from the inside. Place the hole of the "T" over the brad on the underside and spread the brad to secure it.

6. Decorate your wagon any way you like, and give your beanie toys or fashion dolls a ride!

YOU'LL NEED:

- Shoe boxes with lids
- Four 1/2- to1/3-inch metal brads
- Large jar lids (about 3 inches across) or a math compass to make circles
- Scissors
- Hole punch
- Cardboard

Optional: If you have a large group and limited time, ask some older kids to help you cut out pieces ahead of time.

If you just can't stop here…
Make a sightseeing train by attaching the wagons to each other with brads! For canopies, tape 12-inch sticks or dowels to each inside corner. Top with another shoe-box lid, or a canopy made of construction paper or pretty cloth.

GODPRINT: Helpfulness

CRAFTING CHARACTER

BIBLE VERSE: *Carry each other's burdens, and in this way you will fulfill the law of Christ* (Galatians 6:2)

Make a pile of small, smooth stones on a sheet of paper. Challenge kids to try to pick up the pile without spilling any of the stones. See how many kids it takes to be able to support the paper and do the job together.

• What happened when one person tried to lift this load?
• What happened when we helped each other?
• What's the heaviest thing you ever tried to lift?
• If you couldn't carry it by yourself, what happened when someone helped you carry it?

A burden is a heavy load. But not all burdens are the kind you can carry with your hands. Some burdens are hard times in someone's life. Maybe you have a friend who has been very sick, or something sad has happened in your family. When that happens, sometimes you feel better if you have a friend who knows what you're going through.

Ask a volunteer to read Galatians 6:2.

• Who wants us to help carry each other's burdens? *(God; Christ.)*

We can help carry these loads. This may sometimes mean carrying heavy boxes, but it may also mean staying up with a sick friend, raising money for disaster victims, or mowing a senior citizen's lawn for free.

Close your eyes for a moment. Think of someone you know who has a burden that you can help carry. When you've thought of someone, open your eyes and look at me.

As kids open their eyes, give each one a small, smooth stone from the pile.

Now you've all got a piece of the burden we were sharing. It's a lot lighter now, isn't it? Tuck this stone in your wagon, and when you see it mixed in with your other things, remember that God wants us to share each other's burdens.

Footsie the Sock Caterpillar

Turn an ordinary sock into an extraordinary caterpillar who's grand to behold, even before his butterfly day!

1. Show kids how to lightly, but firmly, fill a sock with fiber stuffing.

2. When the sock is full, stitch it shut by using a drawstring stitch all the way around the sock opening. If most of the kids are young, you may want to ask an adult helper to do this. Older kids may want to try sewing their own socks. Make wide "in-and-out" stitches on the very end of the opening, pulling thread tightly to close, and knotting it securely.

3. Set a pile of rubber bands where kids can reach them. Place rubber bands around the sock about every three inches to create segments.

4. For mouths, have kids cut out pieces of red felt. Make sure they are big enough to cover the drawstring hole and glue it there. Add the wiggly eyes.

5. Show how to run a chenille wire through the head for antennae. Coil the ends.

6. Run chenille wires through the bottom of the caterpillar between each segment and turn out the wire for feet.

YOU'LL NEED:

- A tube-type trouser sock (no heel) for each child
- Rubber bands
- Fiber stuffing
- Wiggly craft eyes
- Chenille wires
- Markers
- Felt scraps, sequins, beads, etc.
- Needle and thread

7. Now the fun part! Kids can decorate Footsie with markers, felt, glitter, or anything else they can think of!

If you just can't stop here…
Make cocoons for your caterpillars from crumpled paper bags taped to long sticks! Or make lo-o-ong centipedes out of girls' tights! See how many legs you can fit on your centipede!

GODPRINT: Purposefulness

CRAFTING CHARACTER

BIBLE VERSE: *There is a time for everything, and a season for every activity under heaven* (Ecclesiastes 3:1).

Caterpillars are slow little creatures. Have you ever watched one move? It takes them a long time just to move a few inches. Maybe you got impatient, wishing the caterpillar could move faster.

Or have you ever seen a cocoon? Pause and let children tell you about cocoons. **Maybe you've watched a cocoon and waited and waited for the butterfly to come out.**

When the time is right, caterpillars turn into butterflies! They're not slow creatures anymore. Now you can't run fast enough to keep up with the butterfly. They flit and fly so fast we can hardly catch them!

• What do you think would happen if the caterpillar tried to become a butterfly before it was time?
• Let's think of some ways that you're like a caterpillar. *(Still growing; have to wait for things.)*

God knows what time is best. Let's read a verse about that. Ask a volunteer to Read Ecclesiastes 3:1.

• How can this verse help you be more patient?

Some kids grow taller faster than others. Some kids learn long division faster than others. Some kids learn to read faster than others. Some are better at sports or spelling or counting money. But remember, God made the caterpillar, and God made you. God has a plan for the caterpillar to become a butterfly, and he has a plan for you, too.

Mystery Door

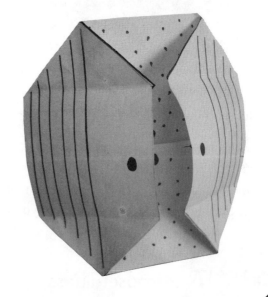

This is one of the coolest paper tricks you'll ever make! It's the door that keeps on opening and opening and opening. . . .

1. Show kids the mystery door pattern piece and explain that they'll need four identical pieces.

2. Following the dotted lines on the pattern, have kids fold each piece at the dotted lines. Put a thin layer of glue on each of the shaded triangles.

3. Lay two pieces parallel, with shaded corners on the outside (see diagram below).

4. Lay the other two pieces parallel, sideways, on top of the bottom two, so that only the shaded gray triangles get glued together.

5. Let the glue dry completely before kids play with their mystery doors.

6. Invite kids to see what happens when they open the mystery door—there will always be another door behind it!

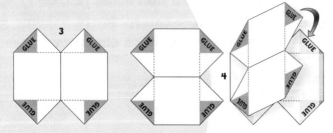

YOU'LL NEED:

- Mystery door pattern
- Paper
- Scissors
- Glue
- Markers

Glue here.

Glue here.

If you just can't stop here...
Make several mystery doors and try making new designs on each panel! See how they change when you open each door!

GODPRINT: Prayerfulness

CRAFTING CHARACTER

BIBLE VERSE: *No temptation has seized you except what is common to man. And God is faithful; he will not let you be tempted beyond what you can bear. But when you are tempted, he will also provide a way out so that you can stand up under it* (1 Corinthians 10:13).

• What do we usually use a door for? *(Going in or out.)*
• What happens with the Mystery Door? *(There's always another door.)*

Sometimes when I go to the store, I try to go in the "out" door or go out the "in" door. Making choices can be confusing! Sometimes we think about doing something that we know is wrong. That's called "temptation."

• Can you think of a time you were tempted to do something you were pretty sure wouldn't be right? *(Kids may not want to answer aloud, but you'll see in their faces if some of them have come to understand temptation.)*

When we face those tough situations, we don't have to do it on our own. Ask a volunteer to read 1 Corinthians 10:13.

• Tell me the words in this verse that can help you when you are tempted.
• How does God provide a way out when you're tempted to make a bad choice?

This verse says that "God is faithful." God keeps his promises to us. If we are tempted to disobey God's way, God will always give us a moment we can use to choose the right thing.

• Can you think of a time when you were able to choose the right thing over the wrong thing?

When you flip your Mystery Doors, remember that God always gives a "door" that leads out.

Matchbox Marionette

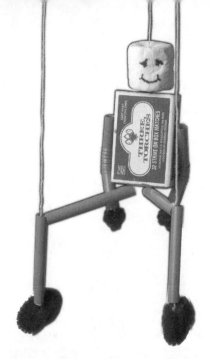

This little matchbox guy is really "on fire for God!" Just watch him dance when you pull the strings!

1. Remove the matchbox "drawer." If kids are punching their own holes, you'll want to supervise carefully. Careful placement of holes is important to proper function of the puppet. Punch a hole in each flinted (striking) side near one end. Punch matching holes in the drawer. Punch leg holes in the bottom side of the drawer. Replace the drawer.

2. Cut the straws into six 2-inch pieces. Run a string through two pieces of the straw, then into one of the leg holes in the drawer and out the other.

3. Continue threading the string through two more pieces of straw. Tie 2-inch pieces of chenille wire to each end of the string and coil them for "feet." Run another string through one piece of straw, into an armhole in the matchbox, through the torso and out the other armhole. Continue running the string through another straw piece. Tie the ends to one-inch pieces of chenille wire and coil the wires into round "hands."

4. Use a pin or needle to poke a tiny neck hole. Push a 2-inch piece of chenille wire halfway through the hole so it fits tightly.

5. Use a needle to run a string through the marshmallow. Tie the string to the bottom of the chenille "neck" and slip the marshmallow over the wire, snugly.

YOU'LL NEED:

- Small, empty matchbox (not a matchbook) for each child
- Two drinking straws for each child
- String
- Chenille wires
- Large marshmallows
- Hole punch

6. Tie strings to the string at the knee joints of both legs. Draw all three strings (two knees, one head) up evenly, making sure the puppet's legs are straight.

7. Make a cross out of plastic straws secured with chenille wire.

8. Tie one leg string to each side of the cross piece and the head string to the long stem of the cross. Tilt the cross side to side and the puppet will dance!

If you just can't stop here…
Make a big marionette, using a cereal-box body, mac-and-cheese-box head, and paper-towel-roll limbs! Use yarn instead of string, and make the cross out of paint stirrers!

GODPRINT: Joy

CRAFTING CHARACTER

BIBLE VERSE: *You turned my wailing into dancing; you removed my sackcloth and clothed me with joy* (Psalm 30:11).

• What body parts did we put on our marionettes? *(Feet, arms, legs.)*
• What can we make the marionette do with these body parts?

Give kids a few minutes to practice making their marionettes move. Then ask them to show you:

• sadness   • excitement
• fear   • thoughtfulness

We can make the marionette's body show lots of different feelings, just as we show lots of different feelings with our bodies. Ask a volunteer to read Psalm 30:11.

• What does "wailing" mean? *(Crying.)*
• Can anyone tells us what "sackcloth" is? *(Special clothing made from camel's hair that people used to wear to show sadness or mourning.)*

• What does this verse say God does with our sackcloth? *(Removes it; replaces it with joy.)*

Show me how your marionette might dance with joy. Let them demonstrate.

• What kinds of things have made you jump for joy?
• What is it about God that makes you the most joyful?

David wrote this psalm when he dedicated the supplies to build the temple. He wanted all the people to know how great God was. Even in our saddest times, God is with us. God turns sadness to joy. God turns our wailing— our crying—into dancing.

Optional: Have kids copy the verse onto small pieces of paper and glue them to the back of the marionette.

Seltzer Rockets

These rockets can't burn anyone, but parental supervision is recommended because they really blast off!

1. Using the construction paper or card stock, have each child make a 5-inch paper tube to fit around the film canister. Make sure the open end of the canister is at the bottom, and that it sticks out about 1/8 inch. Let kids tape the paper to the canister securely.

2. Cut a 3-inch circle out of construction paper and cut a straight line to the center. Roll the paper into a cone shape that will serve as the nose of the rocket. Tape or glue it to the end opposite the canister.

3. Cut three triangles out of construction paper to make wing-fins for the bottom of the rocket. Tape them on.

4. Make a little ring of tape, sticky side out, and put it on the inside of the lid. Stick the seltzer tablet to the tape.

5. Pour a little bit of water into the rocket canister—until it's about 1/4 full.

6. Find a flat place outside for the launching pad. Line the kids up for a group launch or let them take turns. When each rocket is ready to launch, snap the lid on the rocket. Quickly turn the rocket over and set it on the launching pad. Stand back!

YOU'LL NEED:

- Film canister with snap-on lid for each child
- Scissors
- Clear tape
- Effervescent (fizzing) antacid tablets
- Construction paper or card stock
- Water

If you can't stop here...
Add streamers to the bottom of your rocket by gluing on thin strips of colorful tissue paper or very light ribbon. Don't use too many streamers—everything you add to your rocket adds weight, and will keep it from going as high as it could.

GODPRINT: Enthusiasm

CRAFTING CHARACTER

BIBLE VERSE: *Shout for joy to the LORD, all the earth, burst into jubilant song with music* (Psalm 98:4).

• What made the rocket launch? *(The pressure from the bubbles made it burst.)*

Bub, bub, bub, bub, bubblin' over. Have you ever found something that you love to do so much that you don't want to stop, even when it's time to eat chocolate cake?

• Tell me about something that you love to do.
• How do you feel when you're doing something that you love?

That's enthusiasm! When you love doing something, you bubble over with enthusiasm. God wants us to be glad about the work that he gives us to do— so glad that we're just bursting with joy. Ask a volunteer to read Psalm 98:4.

• How do you show it when you feel enthusiastic about something? Do you ever shout for joy?
• What does "jubilant" mean? *(Joyful. Shout for joy.)*
• What makes you the most excited about God?

Your rocket launched because the bubbles in the canister caused it to burst. It just couldn't help but take off! In order for us to "burst" with jubilation, we need to be excited—to realize what a great thing it is to be saved from our sins and to be able to speak personally to God! God's Spirit bubbles up inside us and make us so glad that we can't help bursting with joy.

Get the rockets ready to launch once again. **Let's launch another round, and as our rockets take off, we'll say as loudly as we can, "Shout for joy to the Lord!"**

David's Harp

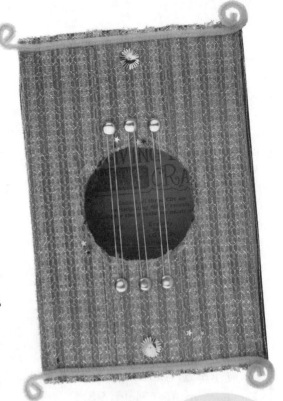

Make your own elegant harp and make a joyful noise to the Lord with strings you can really pluck!

1. Close the box and cover it with construction paper measured to fit (use white glue).

2. Place a 4-inch circle pattern (you can use a jar lid or a compass) in the very center of the box. Trace the shape, poke a hole in the circle on the box and cut it out.

3. Set out gold lace, glitter and craft jewels and let kids design decorations for their harps.

4. Hot glue three spools in a straight line above the hole and three below. Be sure they are evenly spaced. The space between them should equal the width of the middle of the spool. Before you hot glue them, you may want to scrape the paper down to the cereal box on that spot and glue directly to the cardboard.

5. When the spools have dried and cooled, stretch each of the rubber bands over a top and bottom spool so that you have six "strings."

6. Make a joyful noise!

YOU'LL NEED:

- Empty cereal box
- Six miniature wooden spools (in bags at most craft departments)
- Construction paper
- Wide gold lace and ribbons
- Chenille wire
- Glitter, sequins, craft jewels
- Three rubber bands per harp
- White glue
- Hot glue gun and sticks
- Scissors
- 4-inch circle pattern (lid)

If you just can't stop here...

Make a timbrel to go with the harp! Glue two Chinet® plates together ("right" sides facing). Using a hole-punch, make holes in the rim. Imagining the plate as a clock will help you place your holes evenly. Starting at "12:00" and "6:00," punch the next holes at "9:00" and "3:00," then evenly between every two holes you've punched. Run a piece of chenille wire through every other hole and attach a "jingle bell," available in craft stores. Attach ribbons through the remaining holes. Now you can dance with timbrel and harp!

GODPRINT: Worship

CRAFTING CHARACTER

BIBLE VERSE: *Sing to the LORD with thanksgiving; make music to our God on the harp* (Psalm 147:7).

Ah, I just love the beautiful sound of a harp, and you're all making some beautiful music. Let's all strum our harps together. Let the kids strum for a minute, then give a signal to stop.

Did you know that the Bible talks about harps quite a bit? Let's look at just one verse. Ask a volunteer to read Psalm 147:7.

• What does this verse say we should do?
• How can we use our harps to do this?

Right in the middle of the Bible is the Book of Psalms. In Old Testament times, God's people used these psalms as a way to worship God. Some psalms tell about the wonderful things God has done for

his people. The Psalms are full of praise to God. When we worship God, we show that we believe that God is worthy of the very best that we can give him.

When we worship God with our harps, we also need to worship with our hearts. We can praise God for the wonderful things he has done for us, just like the people in Old Testament times.

Let's make up our own psalm of thanksgiving to worship God and make music on our harps.

Invite the kids to take turns saying something that they're thankful for. After each turn, have everyone strum a harp three times and say together, "We thank you, God."

Finger Puppet Theatre

This simple little theatre has a real curtain you can raise and lower with the turn of a knob!

1. Ask kids to carefully remove the tops of each box.

2. Show kids how to turn the box upside down and draw a large rectangle on the front, leaving two inches at the top, 1 1/2 inches at the sides, and at least five inches at the bottom (the open end). Cut out the rectangle.

3. Cover the box with construction paper.

4. Cut a piece of fabric so it's wider than the hole in the box, and a couple of inches longer.

5. Glue the top edge of the fabric around a skewer.

6. Poke a small hole in each side panel of the box, an inch from the top, and 1/2-inch from the front. From inside the box, push the two ends of the skewer through the holes and let the fabric hang over the open rectangle. It's a curtain for the stage.

7. Glue pony beads to each end of the skewer to cover sharp points and to keep the skewer from slipping out either side.

YOU'LL NEED:

- 9 oz.-14.5 oz. cereal box for each child
- Rulers
- Scissors
- Construction paper
- Glue
- Washable markers
- Skewers
- Pony beads
- Fabric scraps about the size of the cereal boxes

8. Roll the skewer to raise and lower the curtain. Draw faces on your fingers with washable markers and let them put on a show!

If you just can't stop here…
Make fun finger puppets by cutting the fingers off a pair of old gloves. The tips of glove-fingers, rolled at the rim, make great winter hats for your finger puppets. Add a tiny pompon to the top of the hat! The remainder of the glove can serve as a matching sweater for your puppet! Make arms from chenille wires poked through the sides of the sweater and wound together, turning the sharp wire ends into a ball to prevent scratches. Make scarves from fabric strips.

GODPRINT: Creativity

CRAFTING CHARACTER

BIBLE VERSE: *Jesus went throughout Galilee, teaching in their synagogues, preaching the good news of the kingdom, and healing every disease and sickness among the people* (Matthew 4:23).

• Why are puppets so much fun?

When we watch a puppet show, we hope we'll hear a good story with some great characters. When we make our own puppets, we can make up our own stories and characters. It's fun to be creative.

• Can you think of someone who you think is creative?
• What do you like about making up your own stories?

Making up stories is just one way to be creative. Maybe you like to draw, or paint, or sing and dance. Those are all forms of creativity, a gift from God, who is the Creator of everything!

• Can you think of any examples of creativity from the Bible?

Jesus is a great example of creativity. God gave him a job to do on earth—tell the good news of God's kingdom. Ask a volunteer to read Matthew 4:23.

• How did Jesus do the job God gave him? *(Teaching, preaching, healing.)*

Jesus didn't teach in a classroom with books and chalkboards. His students didn't sit at desks or tables. Jesus had a creative classroom! He went out to where the people were and he told them stories. The kind of story Jesus told is called a parable, to help people understand things that are hard to understand without a story.

You can make up stories to tell the good news of God's kingdom, too! And using your fingers as characters, you can perform your stories in your Finger Puppet Theatre! Go ahead and make up a great story, or tell a real-life story about how Jesus helped you in some way!

Cereal Box Puppets

You've heard of bag puppets. But how 'bout a box puppet? These are lots more fun and just about as easy to make!

1. Have kids tape the top panels of the boxes closed. Cut the boxes evenly across the front and side panels and crease the back panel so the box halves fold together, back-to-back. What were once the top and bottom panels are now parts of the face of the puppet!

2. Help kids measure the face and draw an oval or circle of construction paper that's slightly larger all around. Cut that piece in half. This forms the top of the face and the lower jaw. Once kids get the hang of it, they can make puppets with faces that have higher foreheads and shorter chins.

3. Show kids how to put the parts of the face together on a flat surface and color in lips along the edge where the halves meet. Draw eyes and a nose, and make hair from strips of construction paper. If you'd like, you can curl the hair by either coiling the strips by hand or by running the strip over a scissor edge the way you curl ribbon.

4. Glue the face halves to the two panels of the box that form the face area. Cover the rest of the box with construction paper.

5. If the box is large, put on a mitten, put glue on the

YOU'LL NEED:

- **Cereal box for each child**
- **Construction paper**
- **Glue**
- **Scissors**
- **Markers**

palm side and thumb and "glue your hand" to the box in "puppeteering position"; or glue a band of craft foam in an arch, over the spot where the hand will be. It will help hold little hands in!

If you just can't stop here…
Make gelatin-box puppets the same way! They're just as cute—only smaller! Use mac 'n' cheese boxes for mid-sized box puppets. Most narrow-sided boxes will do. Try using yarn for hair. Make a whole family with different sized boxes!

GODPRINT: Hope

CRAFTING CHARACTER

BIBLE VERSE: *He will yet fill your mouth with laughter and your lips with shouts of joy* (Job 8:21).

• What's your favorite part of a puppet?
• The puppets we made have mouths that move. Why is that important to a puppet?

Think about how much you can tell about a person by looking at the person's mouth. Use your own lips to show me:

• **a happy mouth**
• **an angry mouth**
• **a sad mouth**
• **a blabbermouth**
• **a surprised mouth**

Have you ever been so sad about something that your mouth drooped? Droop your own mouth expressively. **Maybe you lost your favorite toy, or had to give away your favorite shirt because you outgrew it, or your pet got sick. Or maybe something sad happened to someone you love, and you're not sure things will ever be the same again.**

When you feel that way, it might seem as if nothing could ever make you smile again. God doesn't forget us in those hard times. Ask a volunteer to read Job 8:21.

• Tell me in your own words what this verse says God will do for us.
• Why is laughter important?

When you work your puppet's mouth, don't forget to fill it with laughter and joy! That will help you remember that God will fill your mouth with laughter and your lips with shouts of joy.

In this chapter

Chapter 4
Lip-Smackin'
Snackables

Play with your food?
Absolutely! At least, when
you're having these these
Lip-Smackin' Snackables
with your favorite group of
munchkins!
A little creativity can make
ordinary snacks taste better,
and they'll add color and
interest to your table settings!

Gumdrop Bouquet

This little bouquet of cookies and gumdrops is almost too pretty to eat. But please do! And be sure to share them with a friend.

1. Cut the gumdrops in half horizontally (separating the top and bottom). Older kids can help you do this while you're waiting for everyone to arrive.

2. Show how to push the bottom half of a gumdrop over the top end of the straw, sticky side up.

3. Place the hole of the cookie over the gumdrop and press down so a small part of the straw pokes through.

4. Stick the top half of the gumdrop on the top end of the straw to hold the cookie in place between the gumdrop halves. Be careful not to push the straw all the way through the top gumdrop—the gumdrop should look like the center of the flower.

5. Place several finished cookie flowers in a pretty vase made from a decorated tin can. Bend some of the straws, and extend others so the bouquet will be more realistic and interesting.

YOU'LL NEED:

- Small gumdrops (or spice drops)
- Plastic bendable straws (preferably green)
- Sugar or shortbread cookies with scalloped edges and a hole in the middle

6. Oh, and please do eat the daisies!

If you just can't stop there...
Fill small, sterilized terra cotta pots or plastic cups with crushed Oreo® cookies. Press the "soil" firmly, then insert one or two of your gumdrop flowers. You may need to cut the straw if the flower is too tall for the container. It's a bloomin' delight! And you can even eat the dirt!

GODPRINT: Friendliness

CRAFTING CHARACTER

BIBLE VERSE: *If one falls down, his friend can help him up. But pity the man who falls and has no-one to help him up* (Ecclesiastes 4:10).

• Tell me a favorite memory of something you did with a friend.
• How do friends help us be happier people? *(Love us, do things with us, cheer us up.)*

Some people have lots of friends. Some people have a few friends, but they're really good friends. It's sad to think that some people don't have any friends. Some people are so grumpy that it's hard to be friends with them. It's easier to find someone else who's friendlier. But what if you're the one who is so grumpy that no one wants to be friends with you? Ask a volunteer to read Ecclesiastes 4:10.

• What does this verse tell you about friendship?
• What happens to the person who has no friends?

• How can you make it hard for people to want to be friends with you?

God wants us to be friendly to other people—even the grumpy ones. It's one way to show God's love to other people. Giving flowers to someone is a great way to show friendship.

• Tell me some times when you've seen people receive flowers. *(When a baby is born, at a concert, Mother's Day.)*
• How do you think giving flowers makes friendship easier?

Now that we've made sweet bouquets of friendship today, we have a perfect way to show friendliness to someone who needs a friend. Think about someone with whom you could share one of your cookie flowers and make a new friend.

Snailspins

Slow down the pace and enjoy this yummy variation of the ordinary peanut butter sandwich while learning the virtue of being patient!

1. Give each child a flour tortilla and some peanuts in the shell.

2. Spread an even layer of peanut butter on the bread, being sure to spread it to the edges.

3. Roll it up like a jellyroll.

4. Slice the rolls into one-inch "snailspins"—snail shells.

5. Using a marker, draw eyes and a mouth on one end of a peanut.

6. Using peanut butter for "glue", stick the peanut on the bottom of the bread shell, and you've got a snail!

YOU'LL NEED:

- Green or white flour tortillas
- Peanut butter
- Whole peanuts in the shell

If you just can't stop here…
Make some sweet and fruity turtles as a complement to your peanut butter snails. Select ripe (slightly soft) kiwi, one for every two persons. Gently scrub the fuzz off the fruit with a clean sponge. Slice each kiwi in half lengthwise. Put a shelled peanut in one end for the head. Stick four peanut halves into the sides for feet. Eat slowly! They're yummy!

GODPRINT: Perseverance

CRAFTING CHARACTER

BIBLE VERSE: *You need to persevere so that when you have done the will of God, you will receive what he has promised (Hebrews 10:36).*

People get in such a hurry! Faster usually seems better. But faster isn't always better. Some things need time.

• Tell me some things that are better if you slow down while you do them.
• What are some things that take a long time to do right?
• Can you think of anything that takes so long that you feel like giving up?

Snails are slow critters, aren't they? If you've ever watched one, you know that it takes a *really* long time for a snail to go from one spot to another. But it gets there! It doesn't give up. Ask a volunteer to read Hebrews 10:36.

• Tell me in your own words what the word "persevere" means.
• Why should we persevere? *(To do God's will; to receive what God promised.)*

God promises that he'll never leave us. He promises to be with us. He promises to guide us. He promises to help us when something takes so long that we feel like quitting. And he promises eternal life. When we persevere in doing the work that he gives us to do, God keeps all those promises.

So the next time you see a snail—or eat a snail sandwich—think about the satisfaction of making slow and steady progress. God gives you everything you need to get the job done.

Marshmallow-Coconut Sheep

Enjoy this little tribute to the biblical symbol of submission! And these little sheep are sweet enough to eat!

1. Show how to stick four toothpicks into one rounded side of a large marshmallow to represent legs. Slide on a mini marshmallow to form the upper part of each leg.

2. Use a toothpick to connect a small marshmallow (the sheep's head) to the large one (the sheep's body).

3. Pinch the sides of the marshmallow head to form ears.

4. Paint the big marshmallow body with honey.

5. Sprinkle coconut all over the honey-covered marshmallows, and you have a fat, woolly sheep! Not exactly leg of lamb, but tasty anyhow!

YOU'LL NEED:

- Large and small marshmallows
- Honey
- Sterile paintbrushes
- Flaked coconut
- Toothpicks

If you just can't stop here…
Make sheep with black legs and heads by using licorice gumdrops instead of small marshmallows! You can still cover the body with coconut flakes, but leave the head and legs black. Use a couple of coconut pieces for ears.

Using this basic idea, you can invent lots of other animals. Experiment with marshmallows and toothpicks and see what you can come up with. How about a giraffe?

GODPRINT: Submissiveness

CRAFTING CHARACTER

BIBLE VERSE: *He was oppressed and afflicted, yet he did not open his mouth; he was led like a lamb to the slaughter, and as a sheep before her shearers is silent, so he did not open his mouth (Isaiah 53:7).*

- Tell me some things that you know about sheep. *(Kids may mention shepherds, flocks, sheep pens, wool, sheep following other sheep and so on.)*
- How do we get wool off of sheep? *(Cut it off; shear it off.)*
- Does the sheep have any choice about getting its wool sheared off?

In Old Testament times, people sacrificed lambs to worship God. The Bible describes Jesus as a lamb or sheep. Jesus is the Lamb of God. Ask a volunteer to read Isaiah 53:7.

- How was Jesus like a sheep in this verse? *(Jesus died as a sacrifice.)*
- Did Jesus have a choice about being a sacrifice? *(He could have saved himself, but he didn't. He died for us.)*
- How hard do you think it was for Jesus to do what God asked him to do?

God's plan was for Jesus to die on the cross to take the punishment that we deserve. Jesus didn't run away. He didn't try to save himself. Instead, he accepted what God wanted him to do. Jesus willingly submitted to God's will, and God used him to save us. Now it's our turn to be willing to do God's will.

- Can you think of some ways that you can follow God's will right now?

Porcupine Muffins

Help kids learn about God's protection while making and eating these tender chocolate-and-cream delights—but be sure to eat the quills first, one by one!

1. Turn the cupcakes or Zingers® upside down so the frosting is on the bottom.

2. Give each child a Bugle® or piece of candy corn. Stick the wide end of the Bugle® in the front of the cake to make a snout.

3. Insert pretzels at an angle, pointing backward from the face, like porcupine quills.

4. Eat them carefully!

If you just can't stop here…
Try making an entire porcupine cake! If you can't find an oval cake pan, make a rectangle cake in two layers and sculpt off the corners. After you frost the cake, let the kids insert pretzel sticks all over the cake, angling backward in the same direction. Leave the "face" uncovered and stick in a waffle cone for the snout. For eyes, use gumdrops or hard candy in black or another dark color. He's almost too cute to eat!

YOU'LL NEED:

- **Moist chocolate cupcakes or Zingers®**
- **Small pretzel sticks**
- **Bugles® corn snacks or candy corn**

GODPRINT: Faith

CRAFTING CHARACTER

BIBLE VERSE: *Stand firm, then, with the belt of truth buckled around your waist, with the breastplate of righteousness in place, and with your feet fitted with the readiness that comes from the gospel of peace. In addition to all this, take up the shield of faith, with which you can extinguish all the flaming arrows of the evil one. Take the helmet of salvation and the sword of the Spirit, which is the word of God* (Ephesians 6:14–17).

• Why did God give porcupines so many quills? *(To protect them from predators; to stick anything that tries to hurt them.)*

Compared to the porcupine with thousands of quills, it might seem as if people don't have much natural protection. Let's find out what God has given us. Ask a volunteer to read Ephesians 6:14–17.

• What does God gives us for protection? *(Prompt the kids to name all the pieces of the armor of God listed in these verses. Read the verses again if necessary.)*
• What can the armor of God protect us from? *(Sin; the devil trying to trick us; temptation.)*
• How does wearing the armor of God help our faith to grow?

The devil tries to make God's people stumble and fall. He wants us to make mistakes and do things that please him instead of pleasing God. Isn't it great that God gives us so much protection against the power of the devil? Our faith is fully protected!

Lion Treats

Kids can learn to tame their tempers and be gentle as lambs while assembling these roarin' good treats!

1. Give each child a pear half to place, hollow side down, in the center of a paper plate.

2. Let them squirt cheese around the edges of the pear.

3. Pass the noodles around and let each child sprinkle some onto the cheese "glue" for a "chow mane"!

4. Add raisins for eyes and a mouth,

5. Place a Bugle®, wide end down, on the pear for a nose. Bite off a piece, if it's too long!

If you just can't stop here...
Why not make a marshmallow-coconut sheep to go with the lion! See the directions on page 63!

YOU'LL NEED:

- Canned pear halves
- Chow mein noodles
- Raisins
- Bugles®
- Aerosol cream cheese spread

CRAFTING CHARACTER

BIBLE VERSE: *My God sent his angel, and he shut the mouths of the lions. They have not hurt me, because I was found innocent in his sight* (Daniel 6:22).

Let me hear a big lion's roar! Encourage kids to roar as loudly as they can. Join in the fun yourself!

Most of us just see lions in a zoo with a big fence between us and the lions. And most of us don't want to get any closer than that! The Bible has a story about someone who got as close as he could get to the lions. Encourage children to tell what they know of the story of Daniel in the lions' den. You'll find the whole story in Daniel 6.

• What would you be worried about if you were in the lions' den?
• What would you be praying for?

The king is this story was a friend of Daniel's. He had been tricked into putting Daniel in the lions' den by some other leaders who didn't like Daniel. The king said, "May your God, whom you serve continually, rescue you" (Daniel 6:16).

• Do you think the king really thought God was going to rescue Daniel? Why or why not?
• Do you think that Daniel thought God was going to rescue him?

Daniel spent a whole night in the lions' den. In the morning, the king came to see if he was still there. Ask a volunteer to read Daniel 6:22. **Daniel was confident in God. He had faith in God and knew that God would keep him safe. Whenever you think about roaring lions, think about confidence—confidence in God!**

Circle Cutter Animal Sandwiches

Ordinary sandwiches become works of art when kids put ordinary shapes together with purpose!

1. Show kids how to cut a large circle (3-inch) with light or dark bread for the head.

2. Cut two smaller (2-inch) circles with contrasting bread and bologna for the muzzle. "Glue" the bologna to the bread muzzle with a little cheese spread.

3. "Glue" the entire muzzle to the head with cheese spread or fruity cream cheese spread.

4. Cut ears from bread scraps—tall ears for a bunny; triangle ears for a cat; long or short ears for a dog.

5. Use raisins for eyes.

6. Use toothpicks for whiskers.

YOU'LL NEED:

- White bread and dark bread (whole wheat or rye)
- Cheese spread
- Bologna
- Circle cutters in various sizes (use 1-, 2-, and 3-inch bottle caps and lids)
- Raisins
- Toothpicks

If you just can't stop here…
Do the same thing using other simple shapes! Make rectangular buildings with square windows and triangular roofs. Make a rectangular car sandwich with circular tires and park it in your mouth!

GODPRINT: Purposefulness

CRAFTING CHARACTER

BIBLE VERSE: *"For I know the plans I have for you," declares the LORD, "plans to prosper you and not to harm you, plans to give you hope and a future* (Jeremiah 29:11).

• What's one of the first shapes you learned to draw when you were little? *(Affirm all answers, but keep kids guessing until someone says "circle.")*
• Once you learned to draw a circle, what other things could you draw?
• Name as many things as you can that have a circle shape. *(Tires, steering wheels, ferris wheels, clocks, plates, machine gears, the top of a bowl, and so on. Have fun encouraging kids to think of unusual things that have a circle shape.)*

A circle is a simple shape, but has lots of purposes. It would be hard to imagine a world without circles in it! If you have a

plan, you can do a lot of things with a circle—like making animal sandwiches! God has a purpose for each of us as well. Sometimes we may wonder what God's plan is, but we can always be sure that he has one. Ask a volunteer to read Jeremiah 29:11 from the Bible.

• What kind of plan does God have for us? *(A good plan; a plan to help us; a plan for hope.)*
• Why is it important to know that God has a plan? *(So we can know he's with us and helping us; so we can try to follow God's plan when we make decisions.)*

When you set out to make an animal sandwich, you had a plan for the best animal you could make. When God made you, he had a plan for you. Remember to look for God's purpose, because you can be sure he has one.

In this chapter

Chapter 5
Fashion Funnery

Making things to wear is a crafting favorite. This chapter offers fashion fun for boys and girls! Nothing frilly—just natural, sporty fun ready-to-wear crafts. And besides being practical, these crafts are inexpensive. Such a deal!

Ants on My Pants— or Shirt!

These diligent-looking ants won't bug kids at all! But watch out! Friends may try to slap them off!

1. Show kids how to cut a cookie shape out of the tan felt and take a "bite" out of it with your scissors. Cut little irregular pieces of dark brown felt to look like baked-in chocolate chips. Using fabric glue, stick the chips randomly around the cookie. Don't be symmetrical or "even." It'll look more real if it isn't perfect.

2. Stitch the cookies to the garments. Older kids may want to try stitching their own. Tuck a cotton ball underneath the cookie before stitching down for a little puff.

3. Have kids run a knotted thread through the underside of the fabric. Show how to slip on three beads and run the needle back into the fabric at the end of the last bead. Encourage kids to make the stitches equal to the length of three beads or your ant will be curled up and limp-looking (short stitch) or disjointed (long stitch).

4. Sew the ants in a line toward the cookie, but not too straight. Have irregular spaces between each ant (see photo). If desired, the top two or three ants may carry tan felt "crumbs" stuck on with fabric glue!

YOU'LL NEED:

- Tiny beads (brown, black or maroon)
- Skinny needle and thread
- Article of clothing
- Felt (tan and dark brown)
- Cotton balls
- Fabric glue
- Scissors

If you just can't stop there...
Imagine an ant-covered picnic tablecloth! You might want to make one of those for yourself! It would be especially fun on big, red gingham checks!

GODPRINT: Diligence

CRAFTING CHARACTER

BIBLE VERSE: *Go to the ant, you sluggard; consider its ways and be wise* (Proverbs 6:6).

- When was the last time you went on a picnic? *(Let as many kids as want to tell about their experiences.)*
- Did you have any problem with ants at your picnic?

Ants seem creepy when they're making a path up your leg, or trying to eat your lunch. But take another look at these hard-working little creatures and you may come to appreciate them. Ask a volunteer to read Proverbs 6:6.

- What is a "sluggard"? *(Someone lazy and slow.)*
- What does the ant do that is wise? *(Use this time to find out what kids know about ants.)*

Usually if you see one ant, you'll soon see a lot more—dozens, maybe even hundreds. If you look closely at an ant hill, you'll find it's much more than a pile of dirt. Hundreds of ants are busy making tunnels and carrying crumbs of food to share with the whole colony of ants. Ants do their work as a team, without having to be told. They work to serve their colony of ants, not just themselves.

Ants are diligent. They work steadily without complaining.

- Why can it sometimes be hard to work steadily without complaining?
- Can you think of some ways you can be more diligent?

When we work steadily and sincerely to do what God asks us to do, we work diligently. We have a lot to learn from the ants!

Personalized Dough Jewelry

Even kids with the most unusual names can have personalized jewelry with this craft! And they'll learn what a good name is really all about!

1. Mix the flour, salt and water in a big bowl. When it seems well mixed, knead it with your hands for about five more minutes. Form small, flat shapes to use as medallions, or make bead cubes if you like. Form holes for string with skewers. In fact, if you do make bead cubes, leave the skewers in throughout the baking to ensure that the holes won't shrink.

2. Invite kids to add alphabet pastas to form a name or a word. Then they'll press letters onto their medallions, or cubes.

3. Place the medallions or bead cubes gently on a baking sheet. Bake for at least three hours at 200 degrees Fahrenheit. Afterward let them cool, remove the skewers, string 'em and wear 'em! You may even choose to glue a safety pin to the back of a medallion, as in the "God Bless America Pin" shown in the photo above!

If you just can't stop here...
Make nameplates using the dough and pasta, or even alphabet cereal! Roll the dough to about 1/4" thickness. Cut a shape for the plate or plaque with a rectangular or circular tin, or use a butter knife to cut out a shape of your choice. If you're going to hang it, use a plastic straw to poke either one center hole in the top, or a hole at each top

YOU'LL NEED:

- 2 cups of flour
- 1 cup of salt
- 1 cup of water
- Wooden skewers
- Alphabet pasta
- Sturdy elastic string or leather bootlaces

corner for tying a ribbon or string. Add the letters to spell out a name, Bible verse or encouraging phrase. You may even want to make a dough flower, animal or person to go on your plaque! Press the items in firmly and bake for at least three hours at 200 degrees Fahrenheit.

When it's cooled completely, you can paint your plaque with acrylic paint. What a neat gift for someone special!

GODPRINT: Integrity

CRAFTING CHARACTER

BIBLE VERSE: *A good name is more desirable than great riches; to be esteemed is better than silver or gold* (Proverbs 22:1).

Let's find out everyone's whole name. We'll go around and each say our first, middle and last names. Make sure that everyone gets a turn. **What great names!**

• Raise your hand if part of your name honors someone else in your family.
• Raise your hand if you really like your name.
• If you could choose any name you like, what would it be?

What is a good name? Tiffany? Justin? Aurora? David? We're stuck with the names our parents gave us. Sometimes we might think it's a great name, and sometimes not so great.

But a good name has nothing to do with the alphabet or what the name sounds like. Even if your name is Goober

Jigglewiggle, it can be a good name if people know it belongs to a helpful, wise, diligent and honest person—a person of integrity! Ask a volunteer to read Proverbs 22:1.

• What does "esteemed" mean? *(Valued, honored.)*
• What's special about silver and gold? *(They're valuable.)*

Having a good name means being a person with integrity. When we have a relationship with Jesus, we're new creatures. God wants us to make choices and choose behavior that shows that we're new creatures.

• Would you rather have a "cool" name and be disliked, or an odd name and be loved and respected?
• What do you hope others think of when they hear your name?

Bead 'n' Brass Indian Bracelets

How ordinary pins seem—until kids combine them with beads to form a patterned bracelet! The beauty comes from the beads alone, but from the contrast to the shiny brass of the pins. It's a study in cooperation!

1. Show kids how to open a safety pin and slip on two beads of their first color. Slip on three beads of the second color, then two more of the first color. Close the pin.

2. Each child will repeat this with 75 to 100 pins, depending on their wrist size.

3. Slip the pins over the elastic so that the beads are showing on the same side and the pattern at the top and bottom ends of the pins matches.

4. When each child has put on enough pins to fit his or her wrist size, place the ends of the elastic together, while the bracelet is "wrong side out." Stitch the ends together and turn to the right side. It's ready to wear!

If you just can't stop there...
This little craft makes incredibly gorgeous watchbands! Buy elastic that's the width of your old watchband. All you have to do is fold the ends of your elastic over and create a slight "hem" on each end. Remove the band from your watch and slip the spring-post through the loop formed by the

YOU'LL NEED:

- 3/4-inch brass safety pins
- Tiny beads in at least two colors
- 1/2-inch wide black elastic (long enough to go around the wrist)
- Needle and thread

"hem." Replace the post (with the new band) in its place on the watch. Do the same for the other side and you have a stylish, elastic watchband!

GODPRINT: Cooperation

CRAFTING CHARACTER

BIBLE VERSE: *From him [Jesus] the whole body, joined and held together by every supporting ligament, grows and builds itself up in love, as each part does its work (Ephesians 4:16).*

• What makes this bracelet cool?
• How would you feel about your bracelet if it had pins but no beads? Beads but no pins? All the beads one color?

The bracelet looks so great because all the parts of it work together. Without the pins, we couldn't put the beads in this pattern. Without the beads, we'd just have a string of pins. Without the elastic to hold it all together, we'd just have a pile of beads and pins!

A group of people working together can do something good—it's a lot like these bracelets. Ask a volunteer to read Ephesians 4:16 from the Bible.

• How can the whole body work together? *(It has supporting ligaments that join the parts.)*

• When each part does its work, what happens to the whole body? *(It builds itself up in love.)*
• What kinds of things help people work together well? *(Different abilities, good attitudes, cooperation.)*
• Can you think of some examples of how people work together in our church?

God gives us all different abilities so that we can cooperate and do something great for him. Instead of doing just what we like to do, we can work together toward a common goal. God's plan is for us to put our talents together, just the way we put the beads and pins together for something better than beads and pins separately.

When people work together—no matter how different their backgrounds and gifts—they can make great things happen! Whether you're an arm or a little toe, the whole body needs your part to work at its best!

Jelly Jewelry

Kids will discover how conviction makes us immovable in our faith, the way these jiggly, gelatin shapes harden into plasticized, stringable jewelry!

1. Heat the 9 tablespoons of water to boiling. Add the three packets of gelatin and stir well. Keep stirring until the mixture thickens.

2. Pour the goo into the lids, add food coloring and stir with a fork.

3. In about half an hour, the gelatin will be firm enough to peel from the lids.

4. At this stage, show kids how to cut out shapes to string for jewelry and other uses. Use a plastic straw to poke holes for stringing. Gelatin shrinks and curls as it dries. Circles curl up like stackable, canned potato chips, and strands tend to spiral. These can be neat effects, but if you choose to keep your creations flat, lay them between two paper towels stretched across a large coffee can. Cut the center out of the plastic lid and snap the lid on the can to hold the paper towel "hammock" for a day or two.

5. You can save the little circles that you used to punch holes, and string them with fishing line, gently. They'll dry into little irregularly shaped, colored beads that make great earrings and bracelets!

YOU'LL NEED:

- **Three packets of unflavored gelatin**
- **Large, flat plastic lids**
- **Food coloring**
- **9 tablespoons of water**
- **Forks**
- **Straws**
- **String**

If you just can't stop here…
Make Christmas ornaments or sun-catchers by cutting out your shapes with seasonal cookie cutters. Punch a hole in the top with a jumbo straw. Dry them between paper towels according to the instructions above. Run a pretty ribbon through the hole after it hardens. It's almost like glass!

GODPRINT: Conviction

CRAFTING CHARACTER

BIBLE VERSE: *And the God of all grace, who called you to his eternal glory in Christ, after you have suffered a little while, will himself restore you and make you strong, firm and steadfast* (1 Peter 5:10).

Everybody up on your feet! Imagine that you're jelly. Wiggle and jiggle, wobble and bobble. Shake your legs and arms to get the kids acting like jelly. Slouch and let your head hang from side to side.

• Call out some words that describe what jelly is like. Keep wiggling!

When you think the wiggles are out of the kids, invite them to sit down.

• Tell me some things that would be the opposite of jelly. (*Encourage them to name firm substances that don't wiggle and that hold their shape.*)

• If you wanted to build something strong and unshakable, would you rather use Jello® or bricks? Why?

Ask a volunteer to read 1 Peter 5:10.

• How are times of suffering similar to Jello®?
• What does it take to make gelatin firm? (*Time. You have to wait for it to harden.*)
• What makes our faith firm and strong, and not wobbly? (*God. Times of suffering.*)

We don't always understand why some of the bad things we experience happen to us. But we do know that God is always there with us, and he uses the hard times to make our faith strong. Over time, wobbly jelly faith turns into strong, firm and steadfast faith. I hope that when you wear your jelly jewelry, you'll think of how God is making your faith strong.

Threefold-Cord Friendship Bracelets

Kids can make and wear these bracelets as a reminder that the strongest friendships are the ones with Christ in the center!

1. Ask kids to cut two or more strips from their favorite old shirt or dress.

2. Have kids trade strips, so that they each have one of their own strips and one strip from a friend. Then give each child a strip of plain white cotton cloth to represent Jesus.

3. Hold the ends of three strips together and tie them in a knot at one end.

4. Braid the materials tightly together.

5. Tie the other end into a knot.

6. Have kids tie the braids around each other's hands. They should be loose enough to roll off and on easily.

7. Trim the excess braid just above the knot.

If you just can't stop here...
Make friendship ropes (for jump ropes, pulling sleds, and so on) by weaving strips that are 2 inches wide instead of 1 inch wide, and as long as you like. If you want a very long

YOU'LL NEED:

- Cotton strips, 1-inch wide by 12-inches long, cut from kids' fabrics
- A white sheet or piece of cloth

rope, simply keep tying new strips to the old as they "run out" during braiding. These ropes are very strong and useful. You can easily sew them into round or oval coils to make beautiful pot holders or even braided rugs for the home!

GODPRINT: Loyalty

CRAFTING CHARACTER

BIBLE VERSE: *Though one may be overpowered, two can defend themselves. A cord of three strands is not quickly broken* (Ecclesiastes 4:12).

Before your time with the kids, braid a length of fabric two or three feet long. You'll also need a strip of plain cotton fabric one inch wide.

Ask for two volunteers to hold the ends of the plain cotton strip. **When I say "Go," I want you to pull on that fabric strip as hard as you can. Let's see how fast you can tear it. One, two, three, go!** If you have more strips, you can let more pairs try.

Now let's try something a little harder. Hold up the braided cord and recruit two more volunteers. **The goal is the same. Let's see how fast you can tear this up. One, two, three, go!** This pair will have much more

difficulty and are unlikely to succeed at tearing the cord. Invite other pairs to try.

• Both strips are made out of cotton fabric. What made the second one so much stronger?

Ask a volunteer to read Ecclesiastes 4:12.

• How is two better than one?
• How is three better than two?
• How many strands did we use in our bracelets?

When we made our friendship bracelets, we included a white strip to represent Jesus. The other strips came from you and a friend. When you have a friend, you feel stronger. When Jesus is with you and your friend, you have three strands—and a cord that "is not quickly broken."

In this chapter

Chapter 6

Tin Can-its

Recycling tin cans is great! And here are some ways to recycle them right in your own home! You and your kids can make desk accessories, toys and ornaments to last for years to come! And in the process, you'll learn a little more about the God we serve.

Perky Pencil Holders

These cool, colorful pencil holders will remind kids that Christians before us wrote us letters of encouragement that became part of our Bible! Their writings can help us be confident in our faith.

1. Wash and dry the cans thoroughly and remove the labels. You can do this ahead of time or have kids help.

2. Show kids how to measure a can from top to bottom. Cut colorful pages from a magazine and trim the width to equal the height of the can. Measuring well and cutting evenly is important. Older kids can help younger ones.

3. Roll each page to the thickness of a pencil. Glue under the edge of the roll to keep it from unraveling.

4. Glue the rolls to the side of the can. That's it! You'll be surprised at how cool it looks!

If you just can't stop here...
You can be more select in your magazine pages and create wonderfully artistic designs! For example, use only shades of blue and align the paper tubes from light to dark around

YOU'LL NEED:

- 16 to 20-oz. cans
- Glossy magazines with lots of color
- Scissors or paper cutter
- Glue

the can. It takes more time and patience, but the result can be worth it! Another idea from the 70s is to make a matching trash can by using a large, cardboard ice cream tub (available at ice cream shops) and full-size magazine pages rolled tight. Groovy!

GODPRINT: Conviction

CRAFTING CHARACTER

BIBLE VERSE: *I write these things to you who believe in the name of the Son of God so that you may know you have eternal life* (1 John 5:13).

• What do you use pens and pencils for? *(Write letters; homework.)*
• What's your favorite thing to write?
• Have you ever had a favorite pencil or pen?
• How do you feel when you need a pencil and you just can't find one?

Pens and pencils are great tools. It's nice to have a great place to keep our pens and pencils so we can find one when we need it.

Writers of the Bible surely valued their pens. And we should be glad they used them! John, a disciple of Jesus, used his pen to give us confidence in God. Ask a volunteer to read 1 John 5:13.

• What does John say was his reason for writing?
• Why is this an important message to give?

John used his pen to encourage the people he wrote a letter to. When we read that letter, the Book of 1 John, we're encouraged, too. Pass out sheets of writing paper or note cards. **Let's use our pens to encourage someone else. Write a kind note, reminding someone of God's love in his Son, Jesus Christ.**

You might want to plan ahead who will receive the encouragement notes. Perhaps you have some senior citizens in your congregation who aren't able to get to church very often. Or maybe some of the kids have an elderly relative in a nursing home and know how much others there would appreciate a note. Consider sending notes to a missionary family who has children about the ages of the kids in your class.

Jar-Ring Picture Frame Ornament

This perky ornament is a great way for kids to share with people they love.

1. Show kids how to place one of the jar rings over a photo and trace a circle around the outside of the area they wish to frame. Do the same for the other photo.

2. Lay one of the rings on the table, topside down.

3. Apply a thin bead of glue around the inside bottom of the ring. Lay the photo on top, picture side down. Add a little glue around the edge of the photo and lay the lid, shiny side down, on the photo. Press firmly. Repeat for the other photo.

4. Make sure kids pay attention to where the top of each photo is. Apply a dot of glue to the rim at the top of one ring. Fold the three-inch ribbon into a loop. Lay the loop in the dot of glue (about 1/2 inch from the bottom of the loop).

5. Apply glue to the entire rim and match the other ring to it (rim to rim, back to back), making sure the photos are upright, with the loop at the top.

7. Cover the seam of the rings with lace, ribbon, or cording, and it's ready to hang!

YOU'LL NEED:

- Two metal jar rings with lids for each child
- Hot glue gun and sticks
- Ribbons, lace and gold trims
- Two photos to cut and frame for each child. Ask kids to bring these in.

If you just can't stop here…

Make a family collection of ornaments with pictures of the whole family.

GODPRINT: Love

CRAFTING CHARACTER

BIBLE VERSE: *Remember not the sins of my youth and my rebellious ways; according to your love remember me, for you are good, O LORD* (Psalm 25:7).

- Stand up if you're the youngest person in your family. *(Ask kids who stand to sit down after standing.)*
- Stand up if you remember an aunt or uncle or cousin you haven't seen in a long time. *(Ask kids who stand to sit down again.)*
- Stand up if you've *never* done something that you knew was wrong. *(No one will stand!)*
- Stand up if someone who loves you has forgiven you for doing something wrong. *(All the kids will probably stand.)*

Love is powerful! Love helps us to remember people we don't get to see very often. Sometimes we like to look at pictures to help us remember our love. You probably have pictures around your house of people your family cares about in special ways. Maybe your mom or dad has a picture of you at work.

Love also helps us forgive hurts and remember good things. Ask a volunteer to read Psalm 25:7.

- What does the person who wrote this verse want from God? (*For God not to remember the bad things but to remember him with love.*)
- Do you think God will answer this request? Why or why not?

The person who wrote this verse knew that he had done bad things—things that God did not want him to do, things that were against God's way. But he wants God to forgive those things and remember him with love. And that's what God does. He remembers us with love and goodness, and because God loves us, we're able to love other people. When you hang your jar-ring ornament, you'll remember this time when we made them together. But you can also remember that God remembers you with love.

Tabitha Pincushions

These cute and easy pincushions will remind kids of Tabitha, a woman in the Bible whose compassion caused her to use her gift of sewing to help the poor. And what a great gift addition for someone's sewing box!

1. Wash the cans thoroughly and remove the label. Add a little bleach when washing to eliminate the smell (or use an automatic dishwasher).

2. Make a plump ball of cotton, and cover at least half of the ball with the circle of fabric.

3. Squirt out a generous strip of glue around the inside of the can, just under the rim. You may also squirt glue on the sides (inner) and bottom. If you're using hot glue, have an adult on hand to help!

4. Stick the ball, cotton side down, into the can, making sure the fabric touches the glue inside. Add lace around the rim with the glue gun and that's it! Grandma will love it!

YOU'LL NEED:

- Small-size cat food cans
- Ruffled lace strip (enough to go around the rim)
- Hot glue gun and sticks OR fabric glue
- Cotton balls or polyester fiber filling
- 6-inch circles of fabric

If you just can't stop here…

Add an elastic band and make it a wristband pincushion! This will only work with the small cans (cat food). Using E-6000® adhesive, glue the ends of the elastic band under the can, forming a "bracelet." Do not use hot glue or regular white glue; it just won't stick.

GODPRINT: Compassion

CRAFTING CHARACTER

BIBLE VERSE: *Be kind and compassionate to one another, forgiving each other, just as in Christ God forgave you* (Ephesians 4:32).

This little pincushion can be very handy to somebody who sews a lot and needs a place to safely store needles and pins. Do you know of anyone who sews a lot?

The Bible tells us about a woman named Tabitha who sewed lots of clothing for people. She liked to help the poor by making things for them to wear.

One day, Tabitha became sick and died. People stood around showing the clothes that Tabitha had made for them. The disciples called for Peter to come at once. Peter got down on his knees and prayed. Turning toward the dead woman, he said, "Tabitha, get up." She **opened her eyes, and sat up! People were amazed to see their beloved friend alive again. Many people believed in the Lord that day.** If you prefer, ask kids to read the whole story from Acts 9:36–42.

Tabitha had compassion toward others. Her feelings of compassion toward the needy caused her to be kind and use her gift of sewing to help the poor. She probably made many more robes after God's power gave her life again! Ask a volunteer to read Ephesians 4:32.

• How did Tabitha show compassion and kindness?
• How can you show compassion and kindness to others?

When you see your Tabitha pin cushion, let it remind you of Tabitha's kindness. Then look for ways to be like Tabitha.

Coffee Can Birdhouses

Help kids show their love for God's little winged critters by providing a feathered family with this cozy, waterproof birdhouse!

1. Cut a 1 1/2-inch hole in the bottom 1/3 of the plastic lid.

2. Glue the spool right under the hole for a perch. Set the lid aside to dry. Supervise use of the E-6000® glue carefully.

3. Spray paint the cans with waterproof enamel, using a large cardboard box to catch the vapors. (Do this *outdoors*, and at least 20 feet from cars or buildings to prevent airborne droplets from marring property.)

4. Let the cans dry according to the directions on the spray can.

5. Using the nail and hammer, punch two holes in the side of each can—one near the rim and one at the other end. The holes must be even so that the birdhouse will hang evenly.

6. Run a piece of twine through one hole and knot the end several times so it can't slip through the hole. Do the same for the other side.

YOU'LL NEED:

- **Large coffee can (with plastic lid)**
- **Hammer and nail**
- **Heavy twine or piano wire**
- **Waterproof enamel spray paint**
- **Small containers of waterproof brush-on paint**
- **Small paint brushes**
- **Empty spools**
- **E-6000® adhesive**

7. Let kids use the paintbrush and paint to decorate however they wish! Add the lids and the houses are ready for tweet little tenants!

Optional: If you have limited time and space, spray the cans ahead of time. Kids will be able to do everything else in an indoor setting.

If you just can't stop here…
Make EZ birdfeeders! Use empty, clean, clear, plastic soda bottles with screw-on caps. Remove the labels, and be sure they're dry inside. Using a razor edge knife, an adult can cut three or four 1/2-inch holes in the sides near the bottom of the bottle. Apply E-6000® adhesive to the bottom of the bottle and press the bottle into the center of an aluminum pie tin. Let it dry completely. Then, use a funnel (or paper cone) to pour birdseed into the bottle. Screw on the lid, tie a piece of sturdy twine around the bottle neck and you have a bird feeder!

GODPRINT: Preciousness

CRAFTING CHARACTER

BIBLE VERSE: *Look at the birds of the air, they do not sow or reap or store away in barns, and yet your heavenly Father feeds them. Are you not much more valuable than they?* (Matthew 6:26).

Today, you're building a house for tiny creatures to live in and be safe.

• Where are you thinking about hanging your birdhouse? *(Bird-safety tip: if you live in a hot area, hang the birdhouse in shade. Remember it's metal, and direct sunlight could create an oven—and poached eggs!)*
• What do you think will make birds want to come to your birdhouse? *(A safe place in bad weather; safety from other animals.)*
• What's your favorite thing about birds?

Hanging your birdhouse is a way to show your concern for the birds God created. God loves the birds that he created. He feeds them with the seeds of wildflowers, and with the worms and bugs in the soil that he made. But as much as God cares for the birds of the air, he loves you even more. Ask a volunteer to read Matthew 6:26.

• What does this verse tell us about God?
• What does this verse tell us about our relationship with God?
• How did you feel about making a place for birds to be safe and fed? How do you think God feels about caring for you?

God cares for the smallest of creatures. And as much as God loves and cares for sweet little birds, he loves and cares for you more, not because you're bigger, but because he created you so you could have a relationship with him. When you watch the birds eating or playing in your birdhouse, I hope you will remember how God cares for you, too.

Tin Can Stilts

Kids can learn about courage with this oldie-but-goodie that even granddad probably remembers!

1. Give each child two large, empty cans of the same size. Show how to use a hammer and nail to poke holes in each side, one-half inch from the bottom of the can. Enlarge the holes with a screwdriver.

2. Measure the length from a child's fist (arms at his sides) to the floor, add a few more inches and double it. This is the length of rope needed for each "stilt." Run the ends of the rope through both holes from the outside and tie large knots on the ends, inside the can.

3. Do the same for the other can.

4. Let kids' imaginations run free as they decorate the sides of the cans any way they like. Use stickers, paint, glitter—whatever!

5. Show kids how to stand on the cans, hollow side down, and walk while pulling up on the ropes. Voila! Tin can stilts!

If you just can't stop here…
Make wacky feet to go on the cans. It's easy! Just take two 12" sheets of craft foam and draw the print of a big foot on each one—try a frog foot, bear foot with claws, or a big clown shoe. Place your can in the center of the foot and trace a circle around it. Draw an X in the circle, to the edges.

YOU'LL NEED:

- Two equal-sized juice or coffee cans for each child
- Hammer
- Nail and screwdriver
- Clothesline or soft rope

Cut on the X with scissors and slip it over the can, almost to the bottom. You can glue the flaps to the can if you like. Decorate your feet with markers and take a walk on the wild side!

GODPRINT: Courage

CRAFTING CHARACTER

BIBLE VERSE: *He makes my feet like the feet of a deer; he enables me to stand on the heights* (Psalm 18:33).

Stand up on your stilts and see how it feels! Let the kids get on their stilts.

• What does it feel like way up there?
• Is it harder or easier to walk on stilts than on the ground?
• What if you could be this tall all the time?

Ask kids to get down from their stilts and set them aside. Gather in a circle.

Remember King David, in the Bible? Even though he killed a lion and a bear—even the giant, Goliath—he knew that he needed God to give him strength. Ask a volunteer to read Psalm 18:33.

• What is special about the feet of a dear? *(Deer and mountain goats can climb to high places because their feet are made in a way that makes climbing safe.)*
• What do you think it means that God makes our feet like the feet of a deer?
• What things help you feel safe when you're standing up high? How does God help you feel safe?

The deer can climb to high places and stand on the edge of a cliff without being afraid, because God gives him what he needs to do it—the right kind of feet. God gives us just what we need to do things that might be scary for us. We don't have to look at our problems as if they're tall mountains that are too hard to climb. We can actually get above them, because God helps us!

Rockin' Maracas

The papier mâché overlay on these maracas muffle an otherwise brassy sound. Kids will love the pleasant wood-like tone. Plan ahead, because you'll need at least 24 hours drying time.

1. Pass around the can openers and have kids remove the top lid of each can (pop-top, or straw-hole side), then wash and dry the cans thoroughly.

2. Put a tablespoon of dried peas, rice or beans (or a combination!) into each can. Tape over the opening of the can with masking tape. Poke a hole directly in the center with a pencil. Gently push the clothespin, "feet" first, into the hole. Caution kids to only push the clothespin in about an inch . Then tape around the area to secure the clothespin.

3. Pour a few cups of water into a large bowl. Add a cup of flour and let kids mix with their hands. If you have a large group, get several bowls going. Keep adding flour until you get the consistency of gravy.

4. Ask the kids to tear strips of newspaper, about an inch wide and a few inches long. Show how to dip the strips in the "gravy," scrape off the excess between their fingers, and drape it around a can. Let kids know they may use pieces instead of strips, and they may apply them to the can in any direction. Just make sure that the papier mâché covers about an inch of the clothespin where it connects to the can. This will help the pin stay put when it dries.

YOU'LL NEED:

You'll need:
- **Small juice cans**
- **Can openers**
- **Non-pinching clothespins**
- **Masking tape**
- **Old newspapers**
- **Flour**
- **Water**
- **Large bowl**
- **Dried peas, lentils or rice**
- **Pencil**

5. Set the maraca on waxed paper and let it dry at least 24 hours.

 6. Paint the maraca with zig zags and dots in bright, festive colors!

 7. Shake, shake, shake!

If you just can't stop here...
Make larger maracas using vegetable cans and the straightest sticks you can find with a diameter of about 1/2 inch. Fill some with tiny pebbles, and others with different seeds for different sounds. If the handles are too hard for the little ones to make, skip the handles and make shakers. You can even make shakers out of bathroom tissue rolls!

GODPRINT: Reverence

CRAFTING CHARACTER

BIBLE VERSE: *The LORD reigns, let the nations tremble; he sits enthroned between the cherubim, let the earth shake (Psalm 99:1).*

Let's give a loud maraca shake! Lead the kids in shaking their maracas as vigorously as they like. Then ask them to set their maracas on the floor and sit in a circle.

• Let's name some things that shake. *(Affirm all the answers kids offer.)*
• What's something good about shaking?
• Can you think of anything that might be scary about shaking? *(Some kids might talk about earthquakes.)*

Let's read what the Bible says about the earth shaking. Ask a volunteer to read Psalm 99:1 from the Bible.

• What does this verse tell us about God? *(He reigns; he sits on a throne.)*
• Who knows what "cherubim" means? *(A kind of angel.)*
• What does this verse say about the earth? *(It shakes. The nations tremble.)*

God is the king over all the earth! This verse talks about the power that God has—power to make the nations afraid of him, power to make the earth shake. That sounds like the whole earth is afraid of God! God doesn't want us to be afraid of him, but he does want us to respect his power. When we remember God's power, we don't think so much about our own power. Then God can show his kingdom through us.

So instead of shaking in fear, let's shake in praise of the king over all the earth. One more big maraca shake!

Lacey Vasey

This is a great complement to the Gumdrop Bouquet on page 58! And while it's about the easiest craft in the book, kids will enjoy it because they can make it as complex as they like!

1. Have kids cut paper or fabric into strips approximately 12 inches by 6 inches—to go around the can. Cover the cans by gluing on construction paper or fabric.

2. Starting from the top of the can, neatly glue a tier of lace around the can.

3. Glue another tier just under the edge of the upper layer.

4. Keep this up until the can is covered with tiers of lace.

5. Fill with a "Gumdrop Bouquet" (see page 58), paper flowers, or a pretty wildflower bouquet you pick yourself!

If you just can't stop here…
If you don't want to use edible flowers, make paper flowers with colorful tissue! Cut the tissue with a wavy or scalloped edge, about 2 1/2 inches wide and as long as you like (shorter pieces make buds; longer pieces make larger blooms). Roll the strip around the top 1/2 inch of a green

YOU'LL NEED:

- Tin cans (15- to 18-oz. size, washed, label removed)
- Several gathered lace strips per vase (approximately 12" in length or more, depending of the size of the can)
- Glue
- Construction paper or fabric
- Scissors

chenille wire, keeping the bottom edge tight, and the rest as loose as you can. While pinching the bottom of the flower, separate the tissue layers to open the "petals." Tape the bottom of the flower with green tape. Add green tissue leaves if you like!

GODPRINT: Wisdom

CRAFTING CHARACTER

BIBLE VERSE: *By wisdom a house is built, and through understanding it is established; through knowledge its rooms are filled with rare and beautiful treasures* (Proverbs 24:3–4).

- What do you think your Lacey Vasey will be useful for? *To hold pencils, flowers, coins, to give as a gift—kids will name all kinds of things.)*
- What did you like best about making your Lacey Vasey?
- Tell me some things we had to be careful about in order to do a good job on the Lacey Vasey *(Measure paper, glue without getting messy, get the rows close together and so on.)*
- How important was it to understand what you were supposed to do? Why?

Our vases are so beautiful! And we can fill them with beautiful things, even treasures. But how will we understand what a beautiful treasure is? Ask a volunteer to read Proverbs 24:3–4.

- This verse talks about a house. We made a vase. How are the house and the vase the same? *(You have to build them both carefully so that you end up with something good.)*
- What are some important words in this verse? *(Wisdom, understanding, knowledge.)*
- Why do we need these things in our lives?

Have you ever thought of your life as a house? We want to build our lives with the same careful wisdom that we use to build a house or a Lacey Vasey. The best news is that God gives us the wisdom we need to build a strong and wise life-house. When you look at your Lacey Vasey and remember how carefully you worked on it, I hope that will remind you to build your life-house with the same careful wisdom.

In this chapter

Everybody loves animals.
These critters are especially
loveable, because you'll make
them yourself! And while
you do, each one will teach
you and your kids something
special about God.

Chapter 6
Bugsies and Beasties— and Bears! Oh My!

Pine Cone Owls

This inquisitive little owl can serve as a reminder to seek the wisdom of God!

1. Turn the pinecone stem-side down. Cut out two small brown felt triangles (this will depend on the size of your pinecone) and glue them, point side up, to the top sides of the pinecone.

2. Cut out small circles of felt, slightly larger than the wiggly eyes. Glue the wiggly eyes in the center of each circle. Glue these to the front of the pinecone.

3. Cut a yellow felt triangle and glue it, point side down, under the eyes.

Sit the owl in a nest made of sphagnum moss—or a real bird's nest, if you have one.

If you just can't stop there…
Use little pinecones to make babies the same way you made the big one! Fill the nest with a mother and two or three little ones for a really neat room decoration.

YOU'LL NEED:

- **Open pinecones**
- **White glue**
- **Yellow and brown felt scraps**
- **Wiggly eyes**
- **Sphagnum moss or bird's nest**

CRAFTING CHARACTER

BIBLE VERSE: *If any of you lacks wisdom, he should ask God, who gives generously to all without finding fault, and it will be given to him.* (James 1:5).

What animal asks a question every time it makes a sound? Who, who! An owl! Maybe that's why the owl has a reputation for being so wise! Asking questions is one way to get answers and gain knowledge. Just think of all the things that an owl must know.

- Can you name some other words that help us ask questions? *(What, where, when, how, why.)*
- What kind of knowledge can we get by asking questions?
- What's the difference between knowledge and wisdom? *(Knowledge means having facts or information; wisdom means knowing how to make good decisions.)*
- Is being smart the same as being wise?

Let's find out what the Bible says about wisdom. Ask a volunteer to read James 1:5.

- How does the verse say we get wisdom? *(It says, ask God.)*

"May I have some wisdom?" This is one question God wants us to ask! You can ask all kinds of questions and get knowledge and information. God is the one who can help you use that information to make wise decisions— decisions that will honor him. I hope you'll think of a place to put your pinecone owl where you can see it often. Then when you look at it, you can remember that if we ask God for wisdom, he gives it to us.

Nutty Bugs

Turning nuts into bugs is just a matter of creativity! Look at the nuts and see if you can imagine bug bodies.

WALLY NUTT SPIDER

1. Gently crack a walnut open, keeping both sides of the shell intact. Remove nut meats. Depending on the ability of your kids, you may want to complete this tricky step ahead of time.

2. Have kids each cut two chenille wires into three equal pieces. Turn one of the shells open side up. Bend the wires around the rim of the shell, so that about 1/2 inch of each wire is actually inside the shell. Show kids how to arrange the wires, three per side. As they work, go around with a hot glue gun and put a generous puddle of hot glue in the shell to hold the wires securely. Caution kids not to touch the hot glue!

3. Put some glue around the rim of the nut and put the shells back together and let it cool completely.

4. Apply a blob of glue in the top (stem area) of the nut. Attach a filbert to the glue to form the head of the spider. Glue peppercorns to the filbert for eyes.

5. Bend the spider legs into arcs.

NUTTY BEE

1. Glue a filbert to the stem area (top) of the pecan. Supervise the use of hot glue carefully!

2. Cut two wings out of waxed paper. Fold and crease each wing lengthwise. Then crush it. This forms "veins" on the wings. Open the wings and smooth them out.

YOU'LL NEED:

- Whole walnuts
- Pecans
- Filberts (hazelnuts)
- Peppercorns
- Popcorn
- Waxed paper scraps
- Chenille wire
- Hot glue gun and sticks

3. Glue the wings to the back of the neck in a "V" formation, fanning out toward the back.

4. Wrap a piece of yellow chenille wire around the bee's neck and clip it with a scissors. Glue the circle together on the belly side. Wrap two more circles of chenille wire around the pecan and glue under the belly.

5. Use a different color of chenille wire for the legs. Cut a 2-inch piece and bend it into a "V." Glue it under the "neck" of the bee. Bend the wire to make tiny feet.

If you just can't stop here…
You can make lots of other bugs and critters. Try making an ant using three filberts glued together. Peppercorns make great ant eyes. And a half walnut shell glued face down on smooth stone makes a great turtle. Use peppercorns or coffee beans for the head and feet. Paint his back green and he almost seems to move.

GODPRINT: Creativity

CRAFTING CHARACTER

BIBLE VERSE: *God made the wild animals according to their kinds, the livestock according to their kinds, and all the creatures that move along the ground according to their kinds. And God saw that it was good* (Genesis 1:25).

- Name as many different kinds of bugs as you can think of. *(Affirm all the answers kids offer. This could be a long list!)*
- What do you think the world would be like if there were only one kind of bug? Imagine every bug is just like every other bug. Would that make the world better or worse?

Let's find out what the Bible says about the bugs of the earth. Ask a volunteer to read Genesis 1:25. **Most of the time when we read this verse, we think about the big animals—cows, horses, rhinoceroses—that walk the earth.**

- Where are the bugs in this verse? *(Every creature that moves along the ground.)*
- Raise your hand if you like bugs.
- How does God feel about the bugs? *(Everything God made was good.)*

When God made the animals of the earth—including the bugs—he was more creative than we could ever imagine! I don't think any of us could dream up so many different kinds of animals and bugs. When God created humans, he made us in his image. That means that we're like God in ways that the animals are not. Being made in God's image gives us creativity of our own. We can use the gifts and ideas that God gives us in ways that bring honor to him. When we make a bug craft, we celebrate that God is the creator of everything!

"Grr-Bear" Baby Food Jars

Kids will be eager to follow this little pompon-head bear's example by trading a ferocious reputation for one that's helpful and kind!

1. With the lid on the jar, show kids how to apply a circle of glue around the perimeter of the lid.

2. Cut fabric circles ahead of time, or set out supplies and let kids cut their own. Center the fabric circle (right side up) on the jar lid and press it into the glue.

3. Glue the large pompon to the top of the jar. Glue two smaller pompons for ears.

4. Cut out a blunt heart shape for the muzzle from the felt and glue it to the head.

5. Glue beads for the eyes and nose, and a teeny piece of pink felt for the mouth.

6. Glue a ribbon around the sides of the jar lid and tie it into a bow.

7. Glue the two leftover pompons to the sides of the lid for paws.

YOU'LL NEED:

- Baby food jars
- 8-inch circle of fabric
- 8-inch ribbon
- 2-inch pompon
- Four 1/2-inch pompons
- Felt scraps
- Beads
- Glue

If you just can't stop here…
Make other animals using felt ears instead of pompons. You can make a bunny simply by adding felt ears (cut 2 marquis shapes, about 2 inches long and 1/2-inch wide). Dog ears can be triangular (erect) or teardrop shaped (floppy). Cat ears are small and triangular and set wide apart. Have fun experimenting and see how many animals you can make!

GODPRINT: Kindness

CRAFTING CHARACTER

BIBLE VERSE: *A gentle answer turns away wrath, but a harsh word stirs up anger* (Proverbs 15:1).

Grrrr! Why be a terror bear when you can be a teddy bear?

• How many of you have had a favorite teddy bear, either now or when you were younger?
• Is your teddy bear scary or cuddly?

Some people think acting gruff and tough like a bear is a sign of strength. But according to the Bible, that's not true. Being kind is a sign of much greater power. Kindness and friendliness are much stronger than anger and grumpiness. Have a volunteer read Proverbs 15:1.

• What happens when we speak gently?
• What happens when we're harsh or unkind?

Imagine! We might think that a calm reply is weak, compared to somebody's angry hollering. But a calm reply is actually stronger! It can help stop an argument quicker than yelling can.

• What do you have to do to keep an argument going? *(Yell louder. Keep on arguing. Stay mad yourself.)*
• What can you do to stop an argument? *(Stop talking. Walk away.)*

To keep an argument going, all you have to do is keep on yelling back. And the louder you yell, the louder the other person yells. And if you say something bad, the other person will say something worse.

But kindness can break the yelling cycle. How? Probably because the loud person realizes how silly it is to yell at someone who is calm and in control!

Bears can be scary, growly animals. But teddy bears are gentle and cuddly. When you look at your bear, remember not to be a terror bear, but a teddy bear.

Money Bunny

This fluffy bunny looks more like a stuffed toy than a bank. That's what makes him perfect for stashing kids' savings for a special offering or a surprise gift for someone special!

1. Have kids remove the plastic lids and set them aside.

2. Cover the sides of the can with white fur, preferably with the nap running toward the back of the bunny. Glue the fur on with hot glue. Supervise use of the glue gun carefully. Kids can be cutting and planning their next steps while you or a helper come around with the glue gun.

3. Turn over a piece of leftover fur so you're looking at the back side. Use the lid and trace two circles. Trace the 1" hole in one of the pieces. Use a tuna can to mark a center hole in the other piece. Cut out the two inner circles. Now you have two fur rings. Glue the fur ring with the smaller hole to the right side of the lid. Glue the fur ring with the larger hold to the "front" of the bunny.

4. Cover the sides of the tuna can with fur and the bottom of the can with white felt. Apply hot glue to the rim and press in place on the hole in the bunny "front."

5. Cut ears from the faux fur and glue to the sides of the head. Cut an ear strip from pink felt and glue to the back side of the fur.

6. Add button eyes with glue. Cut out cheeks from white

YOU'LL NEED:
- Small coffee can and lid for each child
- Tuna cans
- White faux fur
- Scissors
- Pink felt, white felt
- Hot glue gun and sticks
- Round, pink buttons
- Scissors

6. Add button eyes with glue. Cut out cheeks from white felt. Trim the fur to a low nap and glue on the felt cheeks. Add a pink felt nose and outline the bottom (only) of the cheeks with pink marker.

7. Glue a circle of fur to the outside of the lid that will be the back of the bunny. Glue on a cotton ball for the tail. Snap the lid on.

8. For legs, glue four cotton balls evenly on the bottom of the bunny.

This bank has no slot, so kids can remove the lid to put in or take out money or keepsakes.

If you just can't stop here…
Make a lamb, too, using cotton balls for fleece! Use spools for legs and paint them black. For the head, add a black inverted triangle fitting to the edges of the tuna can. Add a pink nose below the center of the triangle. Make white felt ears (ovals) and glue them on. Not ba-a-ad!

GODPRINT: Stewardship

CRAFTING CHARACTER

BIBLE VERSE: *Dishonest money dwindles away, but he who gathers money little by little makes it grow* (Proverbs 13:11).

Stewardship is kind of a big word. Does anyone know what it means? (Listen to responses.)

Stewardship means we realize that everything we have comes from God, so we want to use what we have to honor God.

• Let's list some of the things that God gives us.
• Is there anything we have that doesn't come from God?
• How can we use these things to honor God?

One of the things that God gives us is money. Shopping can be great fun! We love to use our money for things that make us happy, don't we? Sometimes it feels really good to spend money—even all of our money. But what does God think about that? Ask a volunteer to read Proverbs 13:11.

• What are some ways that God gives us money. *(Jobs for grown-ups; allowance; gifts.)*
• How hard is it for you to save money to make it grow?
• What are some ways to use money wisely?

This little money bunny bank can help you have good stewardship. When you get allowance, or a gift, or extra money for doing chores, think about putting it in this bank. You can save it for something special. Or you can use the bunny as a safe place to keep your money while you think about how God wants you to use your money.

Chicken Lips Birdbeak Mask

This bird-beak mask opens and closes with the kids' own mouths! But be careful, little beak, what you say!

1. Fold a sheet of yellow construction paper in half.

2. Draw a triangle on the folded sheet, 5 inches on each side. Cut out the triangles.

3. Punch holes in two corners of each triangle and cover both sides of each hole with reinforcements.

4. Tie a 10-inch piece of elastic to both corners of one of the triangles to form a neck strap. Do the same for the other triangle.

5. To wear the beaks, place one triangle under the chin with the elastic band around the top of the head. Place the other triangle over the bridge of the nose and wear the elastic band around the back of the head. As kids open and close their mouths, the beaks will open and close.

6. Using the marker, draw two nostrils on the top beak. Rawk! It's done!

If you just can't stop here...
Try making other masks using the same principle! A duck bill is the same as a chicken beak, only the beak should be rounded. You can make an alligator snout from poster board

YOU'LL NEED:

- Yellow construction paper
- Round paper reinforcements
- Elastic string
- Hole punch
- Marker

cut into two pieces about 6" x 12". Zig-zag the edges of the jaws to make 1-inch teeth, and bend them down on the upper jaw; up on the lower jaw. Draw small, donut-like nostrils near the outer edge—if they're near the face it will resemble a birdbeak instead.

For more variety in your masks, make pig snouts from paper cups with nostrils drawn on the bottom—no bottom jaw is necessary. You may also use the cups for mice, dogs, bears, and so on by adding pompon noses and chenille wire whiskers where needed. Your class will be a regular zoo.

GODPRINT: Self-control

CRAFTING CHARACTER

BIBLE VERSE: *Do not let any unwholesome talk come out of your mouths, but only what is helpful for building others up according to their needs, that it may benefit those who listen* (Ephesians 4:29).

Squawk! Squawk! How noisy a flock of chickens can be! And how noisy a bunch of kids can be when they get too excited. And how about grown-ups? Yes, grown-ups can be noisy, too. People of all ages can say things they shouldn't. We all need to watch our mouths.

When we put on these masks, the beaks will only move when we make them move by opening our mouths. No one else can make your beak move. Only you can. And only you can make your own mouth move. Only you can make yourself talk.
Ask a volunteer to read Ephesians 4:29.

• Unwholesome talk is words that hurt other people. What kind of talk can hurt other

people? *(Kids may mention gossiping, lying, criticizing, sassing, using bad language.)*
• What kind of talk is helpful for building up other people? *(Compliments, good jokes, saying something kind, encouragement.)*

Ask kids to put on their beaks. **I'm going to say some sentences. If you think what I say is "helpful talk," bob your heads.** Demonstrate. **If you think what I say is "unwholesome talk," squawk your beak. Ready?**

• I want that! Give it to me!
• Here, have half of my cookie.
• What a dumbbell! He's such a jerk.
• Mom, can I help you with anything?
• It's my turn to watch TV. You have to get out of here.
• I think Mrs. Watson could you use someone to cut her grass.

Good squawking and good bobbing! When you put your beak on at home, let it remind you to be careful what you say.

Dragonfly Magnets

This is not your ordinary clothespin magnet—this little dragonfly looks like he could flit right out of a misty, summer morning in the bog! And he's easier for kids to make than he looks!

1. Glue the large pompon to one side of the clasping end of the clothespin.

2. Cut a magnet strip to fit the length of the clothespin and glue it to the opposite side of the pompon head, the underside of the dragonfly.

3. Cut a 4-inch length from the plastic straw. Pinch one end of the straw together and cut the end into a point, starting two inches from the end. The straw will be split. Cut the bottom "point" off.

4. Holding the straw with the longest side up (the "removed" side down), make a 2-inch slit on the underside of the other end of the straw.

5. Slip the slit end of the straw over the handle end of the clothespin (top side). Glue it in place. You may need to clamp another clothespin over it to press down the rounded side for a good adhesion.

6. Cut the wire into two 2-inch pieces. Carefully glue a tiny lime green pompon or bead to one end of each. Glue the other ends into the pompon head, forming antennae!

7. Glue wiggly eyes to the pompon head.

YOU'LL NEED:

- Clothespins (pinching variety)
- Lime-green plastic straws
- Lime-green pompons (1/2 inch)
- Iridescent cellophane wrap
- Wired string or chenille wire
- Lime-green beads or tiny pompons (1/4 inch)
- Magnet strips or sheets
- Tacky glue
- Small wiggly eyes

8. Now for the pretty part! Cut a 4-inch square from a sheet of iridescent cellophane. Fold it in half. Cut out a heart shape, but leave the bottom flat, about one inch wide, rather than making a point. Place the flat edge along the fold and cut around the shape through bother layers. Now you have two sets of wings! Crumple the wings to create veins, then glue the first set of wings near the top hinge of the clothespin. Pinch the center of the second pair and glue behind the first pair.

If you just can't stop here…

Make adorable dragonfly costumes using iridescent cellophane sheets for wings! Just cut the corners of a cellophane sheet to round them. Pinch the sheet together to make a "bow." Secure the center with a twist of chenille wire. Pin the wings to the back of the child's collar. For antennae twist a chenille wire in half around a plastic headband. Twist it tightly into a single antenna and top it with a perky pompon! Do the same for the other side. With radar in place, your dragonfly is ready for take off!

GODPRINT: Wonder

CRAFTING CHARACTER

BIBLE VERSE: *Sing to him, sing praise to him; tell of all his wonderful acts* (1 Chronicles 16:9).

- Did you ever wonder how God made bugs?
- What ingredients do you think he used?
- What did you use to make your dragonfly?
- How is your dragonfly different from a real one? What makes that difference?

God didn't use play dough, or even clothespins and glue to make real dragonflies. He created dragonflies—and the whole the world—by his Word! He spoke, and it was so! God's creation is a wonder! No one on earth can make something from nothing the way God can.

Ask a volunteer to read 1 Chronicles 16:9.

- If you were making a list of all the wonderful things God has done, what would be on your list?

- How is the dragonfly an example of God's wonderful acts?
- If you had to choose one thing that is the most wonderful thing God has done for you, what would you say?

We say that God is wonderful! That's because he makes us wonder! We wonder how he made dragonflies and other bugs. We wonder how he made space. We wonder how he made the rain forest. We wonder how he did the miracles we read about in the Bible. Wow! We can't explain all these things, but we can praise God for them.

Wonder is a good thing! It's good to be amazed that our God is so great! Then we admire his power and magnificence. That helps to keep us humble before him and it helps to keep us trusting that he knows what is best! He is a wonderful God!

INDEX OF GODPRINTS

INDEX OF SCRIPTURE REFERENCES